THE

T0114181

BLACK CLERGY'S

MISGUIDED WORSHIP

LEADERSHIP

PETITION: NO MORE IDOL GODS FOR BLACK PEOPLE

Christopher C. Bell Jr., Ed.D.

Order this book online at www.trafford.com
or email orders@trafford.com

Most Trafford titles are also available at major online book retailers.

© Copyright 2010 Christopher Bell, Jr.
All rights reserved. No part of this publication may be reproduced, stored in a retrieval
system, or transmitted, in any form or by any means, electronic, mechanical, photocopying,
recording, or otherwise, without the written prior permission of the author.

Printed in Victoria, BC, Canada.

ISBN: 9781-4251-7806-2 (Soft Cover)
ISBN: 9781-4251-7807-9 (eBook)

*Our mission is to efficiently provide the world's finest, most comprehensive
book publishing service, enabling every author to experience success.
To find out how to publish your book, your way, and have it available
worldwide, visit us online at www.trafford.com*

Trafford rev. 3/8/10

 www.trafford.com

North America & international
toll-free: 1 888 232 4444 (USA & Canada)
phone: 250 383 6864 ♦ fax: 812 355 4082

Other books by Christopher C. Bell Jr.

Lt. Williams on the Color Front
ISBN# 1-4137-6177-1
A novel about a young Negro lieutenant's experiences in an all white infantry regiment in the 1950's when the U.S. Army began testing to see if black officers could supervise white soldiers

The Belief Factor and the White Superiority Syndrome
ISBN# 1-58500-250-X
A treatise on how and why belief in the divinity of Jesus Christ, Christianity's white male, savior of the world idol, subliminally promotes a harmful white superiority syndrome in non-white people

Soldiers Do Reason Why . . .
ISBN# 0-8059-3867-2
Poems about military life, self confidence, and soldiering

About this Book

The Black Clergy's Misguided Worship Leadership

Citing cogent historical, educational, and behavioral reasons, Dr. Bell explains why the black community's worship of Jesus Christ, the ancient Roman, Made in Nicaea, Constantine-certified, white male, Christian idol is misguided "white male worshipping" that subliminally afflicts many black people with a debilitating white superiority syndrome. He also explains how "white male worshipping" is a subliminal underlying cause of black adolescent low academic achievement motivation and that such worship emotionally emasculates and angers many young black men who react in ways that lead to high rates of recalcitrance, delinquencies, violence, crime, and incarceration. Dr. Bell petitions black clergy and secular leaders to stop worshipping Jesus Christ, and start teaching black people a *new Christianity* that espouses a *"worship only God, the source and sustainer of life"* message and honors but does not worship "Prophet Jesus." He explains why the *new Christianity* is a necessary remedy in liberating black people from the damaging psychological effects of their white-male worshipping folkways, and mediating downward the high rates of violence, crime, and incarceration among young black men.

Acknowledgements

I am beholden to many people who helped me to write this book, but as a seasoned educationist* I take full responsibility for the arguments and conclusions noted herein. I am beholden to New Testament Bible scholars, black psychologists and sociologists, disruptive high school students, secular black professionals, urban school teachers and concerned parents. In many ways they all contributed information and insight, ideas and theories, and problem scenarios and solutions that are the dots I have connected to explain how the black clergy's worship leadership of Jesus Christ, an ancient Roman, white male, idol is misguided and subliminally contributes to the plight and plunge of many young black men toward low self-esteem, self-abuse, violence, crime, and incarceration.

Christopher C. Bell Jr., Ed.D.

*An educationist is one who uses the theories and practices of institutional management and supervision, pedagogical planning and delivery, behavioral science, and policy development to analyze educational systems, in order to understand the inner workings of interrelated sub-systems such as management practices, quality and delivery of instructional services, assessment of intended student outcomes, personnel policies, organizational climate, environmental setting, and self correcting mechanisms.

POINTS . . .

"Fairest Lord Jesus, Ruler of all Nations . . ." **(Words of a Baptist hymn)**

"From slavery to now, black people have placed their trust and faith in Jesus Christ as their God and their Lord and Savior; a Savior who is on the side of the slave and the downtrodden." **(Black clergy member A)**

"Jesus, my Savior, my Love, my Comforter . . ." **(Words of a song sung by a black woman at a church sponsored gathering)**

"Take the world, Lord! Just give me Jesus! Just give me Jesus!" **(A black woman's emotional adoration of Jesus Christ during a Sunday morning church service)**

"These young black criminals don't go to church any way, so how are they suppose to be affected by what we preach?" **(Black clergy member A)**

"The pictures and art in the church factually portray the historical characters involved in the Bible story. Facts are facts." **(Black clergy member B)**

"My master is a Jewish Carpenter." **(Bumper sticker on a truck driven by an elderly black man)**

"Black people have historically seen themselves in the role of the oppressed and having Jesus Christ as their Lord and Savior brings them comfort." **(Black**

clergy member C)

"I know in my heart that can't no virgin have a baby, but I'm going to be Christian until I die." **(Black man at a historical society meeting)**

"Black people are primarily fundamentalists. They have not heard about the Nicene Council or the Chalcedonian Council and they couldn't care less." **(Black clergy member D)**

"To talk against the concept of Jesus Christ as a God would not be in the best interest of black people. It would be more beneficial to black people if we just let sleeping dogs lie and don't stir up controversy." **(Black clergy member D)**

"I must tell Jesus. I must tell Jesus. I cannot bear my burdens alone . . ." **(Words of a Baptist hymn)**

"Oh Happy day, O happy day, when Jesus washed my sins away . . ." **(Gospel song)**

"Jesus is all the world to me, my Life, my Joy, my All . . ." **(Words of a Baptist hymn)**

"My faith looks up to thee, sweet Lamb of Calvary, Savior Divine." **(Words of a Baptist hymn)**

"Oh, to be kept by Jesus, Lord, at thy feet I fall. I would be nothing, nothing , nothing. Thou shall be all, all, all." **(Words of a Baptist hymn)**

"Thru the long night-watches, May Thine angels

spread, Their white wings above me, Watching round my bed." **(Words from "Now the Day is over," a song from a Baptist hymn)**

AND COUNTERPOINTS

"This book (The Black Clergy's Misguided Worship Leadership) is a defiant publication that states that white idols have afflicted blacks with a debilitating white superiority syndrome. . . . The evidence supporting the theories of this book is confirmed for the most part by both black and white experts alike. . . . All in all this is a provocative, insightful book that has been conceived to inspire thought and possible action. . . . But the black church will not change easily." **(Robert Fleming, author, editor, journalist, and book reviewer for AALBC.com)**

"Following the religious teachings of their traducers, Negroes do not show any more common sense than a people would in permitting criminals to enact the laws and establish the procedures of the courts by which they are to be tried." **(Carter G. Woodson, Ph.D., educator and author)**

"Christianity portends that black men bow down and worship a white male as Lord and Savior and white men bow down and worship their own likeness." **(Na'im Akbar, Ph.D., psychologist, professor, author)**

"To be black and accept consciously or

unconsciously the image of God as a white man is the highest possible form of self-negation and lack of self-respect . . ." **(Francis Welsing, M.D., general and child psychiatrist, author)**

"If people all over the world worshipped a white, blond, female as 'Our Lady and Savior of the world,' what would be the worshipful adorations offered during Sunday worship services, and by whom? And how would this change the relationship between black men and women?" **(Christopher Bell Jr., Ed.D., educationist, author)**

"White racist American society . . . generally leaves but a few outlets for the release of societally provoked black male rage; all inappropriate. They (the few outlets) include the abject submission to oppression, narcosis by drugs or religion, deliberate ignorance, criminality, and attacks on other black males or on himself (homicide)." **(*Black on Black Violence*, p. 156; by Amos Wilson, Ph.D., psychologist, author)**

" And Nebuchadnezzar the king made and set up an image of gold and ordered all the people to fall down and worship it." **(Book of Daniel: 3: 1-5, Old Testament, Holy Bible)**

". . . By the decision, the Council of Nicaea created the literally fantastic Jesus of faith and adopted the pretense that this was a historically accurate rendering . . . producing a world of Christianity where a code of belief (the Nicene Creed) was held in common.

Anything different was to be deemed heresy."
(Michael Baigent, M.A., religious historian, author)

"Dr. Bell, your book has hit on the truth, which is so obvious that we have all missed it. Of course the God and Jesus of Constantine's Holy Roman Church are all about white men. And white men only. If you need to worship a God or something outside of your inner being than it should look like you. I can't agree more with your hypothesis." **(Bonnie Lange, Publisher and Editor, Truth Seeker Journal)**

"Christopher C. Bell Jr. has written a bold, powerful and courageous book that has been waiting for someone to write. This book demonstrates that only an Afrocentric approach that unlocks the potential of the African person can make an effective transformation in the lives of black people. No white Jesus can save black folk; we are essentially on our own." **(Molefi Kete Asante, Ph.D., author of "An Afrocentric Manifesto," Professor, Department of African American Studies, Temple University)**

The Black Clergy's Misguided Worship Leadership

Table of Contents

Foreword

Why write this book now?

Background:

Year after year many experts, scholars, and social commentators have written well documented studies and reports affirming that young black males experience higher rates of incarceration, joblessness, drug addiction, high school drop-out, low academic achievement, and mental illnesses in comparison to their white male counterparts. In this book, these higher rates of behavioral and situational outcomes are referred to as the "societal plight and plunge problem" of young black men.

Over the years, many of these studies concluded that poverty and white racism were major underlying factors that contributed to the "plight and societal plunge problem" of young black men. Many of these studies prescribed programs and activities to counter the apparent negative effects of poverty and white racism. Yet, over the years, in spite of several prescribed and implemented programs, there have been increases in the rates of incarceration, drug addiction, violence, and other anti-social behavior among young black males.

After many years as an educationist who has studied, observed, worked with or conversed with black adolescents, young black men, teachers, educators, parents, and preachers, **this author has concluded that the version of Christianity presently taught by the black clergy to black people is itself a major, subliminal, contributing factor to the societal plight and plunge of many young black men toward incarceration.** My assessment of the scope, depth, and present trend of this societal plight and plunge problem compels me to speak out NOW about my observations and conclusions in an attempt to help black people move themselves toward psychological liberation from white superiority syndrome afflictions (which we'll describe in chapter one) and to mediate downward the high rates of violence, crime, and incarceration among young black men. And so:

Now is the time to call black people's attention to their urgent need for more self-knowledge and self-understanding by providing them with information that will explain to them why and how they have learned to think of themselves as inferior to white people;

Now is the time to explain to black people that their present version of Christianity was composed and refined from a variety of existing Christian beliefs by ancient Roman church bishops who were approved (certified) by the Roman emperor Constantine, and that the composing and refinement process resulted in the administrative promotion of "Prophet Jesus" from the status of a crucified Jewish prophet to the status of a Roman, white male, idol god, named "Jesus Christ";

Now is the time to inform black people of the subliminal, negative, mental and emotional effects of their Constantine-certified Christianity on them and why their worship of Jesus Christ, the white male, Roman idol is tantamount to "white-male worshipping" which, in conjunction with other societal factors, spiritually emasculates and intuitively angers many young black men who react in ways that lead to high rates of recalcitrance, delinquencies, crime, and incarceration;

Now is the time to describe the actions that black people must take in order to gain a sense of self-appreciation, spiritual uplift, authentic manhood and womanhood, and psychological freedom. The action required is that black clergy and secular leaders work together **to stop** Constantine-certified, white-male worshipping Christianity, **and start** teaching black people a *new Christianity* that espouses a "*Worship only God the source and sustainer of life*" message and honors but does not worship Prophet Jesus. With this *new Christianity*, black people may begin freeing themselves from the harmful mental and behavioral effects of their white-male worshipping folkways;

Now is the time to simply speak the truth because the world is too dangerous to do otherwise. One of these truths is that most incarcerated young black men acquired their personality traits while maturing inside black communities. This fact suggests that black people should look closely at themselves and at what they are doing, and how they may be contributing to the high rates of violence and incarceration among young black men. Now is the time to look closely at what "white male worshipping" has done to or for young black men and women.

This book addresses all the above urgencies and considerations.

"This book is about grass root advocacy. Dr. Bell argues forcefully that a white male Christ causes black males to suffer by devaluing their blackness and 'Prophet Jesus' embodies the personality traits young black males can relate to in improving their lives. He challenges the black clergy to take on his sense of urgency. Dr. Bell's vision sits well with contemporary psychological research that stresses 'implicit relational knowing' in the realm he calls subliminal personality development." **(Michael J. Papantones, Ed.D., Psychologist, Family Therapist)**

Chapter 1

The Black Child's Educational Environment and The Black Church

Introduction:

This chapter explains how the educational environment of black children and the religious teachings of the black church work together to provide children with ways of defining themselves and interpreting the world.

The Educational Environment of the Black Child:

A schematic of the black child's educational environment is sketched on the next page. This schematic shows many of the societal/environmental factors and institutions that teach black children what they should know about their social circumstances so that they may learn to cope, adapt, survive, and perhaps succeed.

Each of these societal/environmental factors may influence children differently depending on the children's previous learning experiences, their differing coping skills and temperaments, their differing sense of who they are and their differing home-taught lessons or home environments.

1

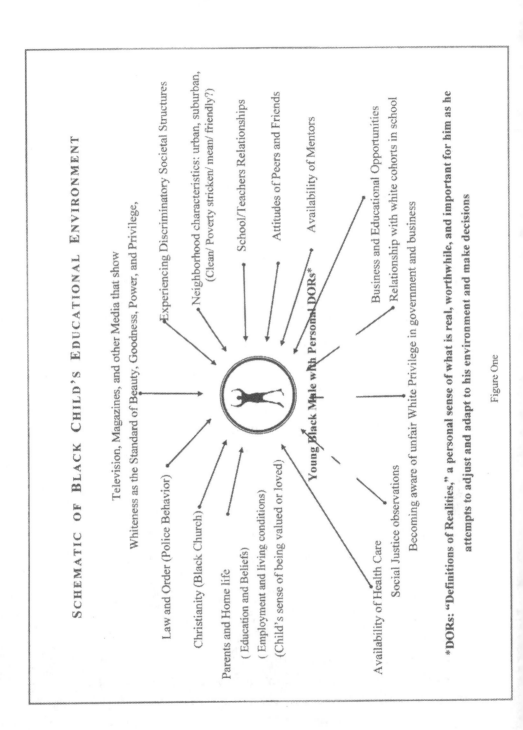

SCHEMATIC OF BLACK CHILD'S EDUCATIONAL ENVIRONMENT

Television, Magazines, and other Media that show Whiteness as the Standard of Beauty, Goodness, Power, and Privilege,

Experiencing Discriminatory Societal Structures

Neighborhood characteristics: urban, suburban, (Clean/ Poverty stricken/ mean/ friendly?)

School/Teachers Relationships

Attitudes of Peers and Friends

Availability of Mentors

Business and Educational Opportunities

Relationship with white cohorts in school

Becoming aware of unfair White Privilege in government and business

Young Black Male with Personal DORs*

Law and Order (Police Behavior)

Christianity (Black Church)

Parents and Home life
(Education and Beliefs)
(Employment and living conditions)
(Child's sense of being valued or loved)

Availability of Health Care

Social Justice observations

*DORs: "Definitions of Realities," a personal sense of what is real, worthwhile, and important for him as he attempts to adjust and adapt to his environment and make decisions

Figure One

2

As an example of how children are influenced by their particular learning environment, those children who live in home environments where their parents constantly manifest feelings of defeat or helplessness, will tend to exhibit the same traits. The only exception to this fact is if there is intervention from another societal factor. The same is true with regards to children's contacts with other institutions. If these other institutions teach them self-respect, responsibility for their actions, or the importance of high academic achievement, they will tend to grow and become self-respecting, responsible, and good students, assuming the teaching process is not interrupted by another societal factor.

Definitions of Realities

The schematic of the black child's educational environment on the previous page shows a drawing of a black child being exposed to various environmental teaching factors. The schematic also shows that the child possesses an attribute labeled DOR, which stands for Definitions of Realities. Definitions of Realities (DORs) is a construct used by this author to encapsulate the how, what, when, where, why, why not, and ifs, commonly used by people to decide how to behave or act. People act or behave according to what they feel is important and significant to their well-being, their situation, and their perception of the likely consequences. **An individual will act or behave based on his personal definitions of realities at the decision-making time.** Definitions of realities include the person's fears, past experiences, self image, values, expectations, reputation, goals, beliefs, etc., and his minute by minute prioritizing of what is important and significant to his well-being, his sense of environmental control and consequences.

In the schematic the child is not a passive object that is simply molded and shaped by the various teaching factors of his educational environment. The child shown in the educational schematic will respond to his teaching environment in the manner that makes sense to his unique, continuous way of defining and prioritizing those things that are important to him. Criminal behavior on his part is not inevitable, even though his environment may be hostile. In the schematic, the black child will decide what to do, and most black children will make law-abiding choices despite the surrounding hostile teaching factors. See Appendix One for a more detailed discussion of Definitions of Realities.

A key lesson learned by black children

At an early age, all children learn to discern and understand who and where they are in the pecking order of their social surroundings. Black children growing up in America learn about America's history, customs, and ideals such as individual freedom, democracy, and equal justice. Black children also learn about America's white racism, white privilege, and notion of white supremacy. White supremacy is the operational philosophy that white people should be in control of the major political, economic, educational, scientific, and military resources in America. Black children also learn that white people have established procedures and processes to maintain control, privilege, and power over non-white people. Most black children will tend to subliminally acquire a white superiority syndrome as a result of being impacted and surrounded by several white supremacy teaching and maintenance factors. **A white superiority syndrome is the belief that white people as a group are inherently, genetically, and esoterically better human beings than black people.** Bell (2000) explained that a white superiority syndrome is a mind and belief phenomenon that affects the thinking of both black and white people. The syndrome prompts black people as a group to harbor feelings of racial inferiority and prompts white people as a group to experience race pride and a sense of an inherent right and obligation to subordinate and control non-whites. Bell indicated that a white superiority syndrome gives many black people a sense of being members of a "low caste" group because of their dark skin color. Conversely, a white superiority syndrome gives many white people a sense of being members of a "high caste" group because of their white skin. In black people, a white superiority syndrome prompts thinking that suggests that white people should take the lead and black people should follow and that white people are superior and beautiful, and that they (black people) are inferior and ugly. By simply living in America, black people will subliminally acquire a white superiority syndrome unless they encounter some type of intervention that neutralizes the normal cultural effects of the white supremacy structures that abound (pp. 29-31). See Appendix Two for more information about the white superiority syndrome.

The teaching role of the black clergy (Church)

The schematic of the black child's educational environment shows that the black church is one of the many societal factors that teach black children. Black people generally think of the black clergy as having the leadership role of community spiritual uplift and of motivating church-goers to adhere to Christian values and principles in their daily interactions. Most black people generally perceive the black clergy as professionals, who via their wisdom, maturity, and sense of "God" will act to help the black community to be morally strong, to gather hope for a better future, and to live in an atmosphere of wholesome fellowship.

The main stream black Christian church is Protestant and fundamentalist. What is Protestant Christian Fundamentalism and what types of pedagogy are involved?

According to Spong (2002), the basic pedagogical religious principles of Protestant Christian Fundamentalism are the following:

1. The inspiration of scripture as the literal, revealed word of God
2. The virgin birth as the miraculous and literal means by which the divine nature of Christ has been guaranteed
3. The substitutionary view of the atonement that was accomplished in the death of Jesus. The affirmation of the saving power of Jesus' blood and the gift of salvation that was accomplished by Jesus' death
4. The certainty of the physical bodily resurrection of Jesus from the dead. The accuracy of both the empty-

tomb and the appearance stories in the gospel tradition.
5. The truth of the second coming of Jesus, the reality
of the Day of Judgment, which would be based on the
record of one's life and the certainty of heaven and hell
as eternal places of reward and punishment.
6. To question or to deny the truth of any of these
listed doctrines or teachings is an act of apostasy (pp. 1,
2).

In addition to the pedagogical religious beliefs listed
above, the black clergy teaches black people to believe
in the content of the Nicene Creed, and believe in the
Trinitarian Dogma; both of which are fully described in
the next chapter. When considered together, this
Creed and Dogma teach that the Christian Godhead
consists of three beings: God the Father, the Creator of
Heaven and Earth; God the Son, who is called Jesus
Christ, the only Begotten Son of the Father; and God
the Holy Spirit.

Another teaching point, although subliminal, is that
over the centuries, in western cultures "Jesus Christ the
Son of God" has been predominantly portrayed in the
likeness of a Western European white male.

Black criminality

Black criminality is a behavioral choice made by an
individual based on his definitions of realities at the
time. Psychologists Clark (1967), Jones (1991), Grier &
Cobb (1992), Wilson (1990), and Turner (1994)
strongly suggest that black criminality in many young
black men is prompted by several psychogenic catalysts
such as feelings of racial inferiority, self-hate,
hopelessness, oppression, psychological dissonance,

alienation, anxiety, ennui, anomie, low self-esteem, frustration, depression, cognitive dissonance, hate, anger, belittlement, and powerlessness. These psychologists also agree that poverty and white racism induce several, if not most of these feelings in many young black men, and thus poverty and white racism may be considered as two underlying causes of the high rates of delinquencies, violence, and criminal behavior among many young black men.

This author argues that the worship of Jesus Christ, the ancient Roman, white male idol, is equivalent to "white male worshipping" and when young black American men are embedded in "white-male worshipping folkways," many of them experience the same negative feelings and anger induced by poverty and white racism. This author argues that the white-male worshipping folkways (worshipping Jesus Christ) presently promoted by the black clergy in the black community subliminally afflicts most black people with a psychologically oppressive white superiority syndrome that cognitively blinds and socially inhibits them. Such worship also spiritually impoverishes, angers, and emotionally emasculates many young black males in the same ways as white racism and white privilege. It is for these reasons that this author argues that the "white male worshipping folkways" of the black community are also underlying causes **of the high rates of recalcitrance, delinquencies, violence, self-abuse, and criminal behavior among many young black men.** To make this point it is necessary that we look closely and analyze the effects of the black clergy's present day

8

teaching and preaching on the psyche (mind) of black people.

The emotional and behavioral effects of the black clergy's worship leadership on black people and black criminality:

This author has for many years observed, conversed with, and listened to many young black men in field and classroom situations; before, during, and after many religious instructional training or activities. Over these many years, this author's educationist faculties, informational probing, and intuitive acumen affirm that the worship of Jesus Christ has several demeaning, negative, and problematic effects on many black people, especially on young black men. This author argues that:

Such worship is misguided. This author accepts as self-evident that the God of the Creation, the source and sustainer of life, as explained by the sages of old, cannot be reasonably and respectfully portrayed as a man, and therefore any worship of a humanoid figure of any kind, type, or personality is misguided. **It is this author's argument that black people must discard any and all of their images of God.** Black people must raise their sense of God to a level that is beyond their ability to imagine or describe or to render as a work of art. Even the Old Testament of the Christian Bible expresses the theme that "Thou shall not make and worship any graven image."

Such worship promotes the notion that God is a white male. When black men worship the image, real or mental, of a white male as their Lord and Savior, such worship is not only misguided but inherently self-demeaning and blunts the concept and realization of authentic black manhood. **Akbar (1991) explained well this demeaning worship when he noted that Christianity portends that black men bow down and worship a white male as Lord and Savior and white men bow down and worship their own likeness (p. 45).** When a mature black male participates in the worship of the image (real or imagined) of a white male, he denies his own authentic manhood and ratifies his boyhood in comparison to white males.

Over the years, many young black men have indicated to the author that they would occasionally attend church, mostly for social reasons, but they were uncomfortable about the thought of worshipping a white God or a white Jesus and they tried not to think about it.

Such worship re-enforces and perpetuates a white superiority syndrome in black people. The white superiority syndrome, as we have already described, prompts black people to accept white people as their superiors in intelligence and in all that is important. When black people worship as their god the image (real or imagined) of a White male, they acknowledge a god-like respect for white maleness. Therefore, white-male worshipping folkways reinforce white superiority syndrome afflictions in black people.

Such worship spiritually and emotionally emasculates and intuitively angers many young black males. For many assertive young black men, the conscious witnessing or participation in the

10

worship of a white male image is tantamount to spiritual and emotional self-emasculation and is intuitively resisted but socially tolerated. In other young black men, the witnessing of white-male worshipping induces an intuitive, sullen anger and disdain toward those who participate in or benefit from such worship and many of these young black men will tend to react in ways that lead to delinquencies, violence, and criminal activity. Although most black males can and do control their anger**, this author argues that there is no sane reason why black people should be exposed to white-male worshipping folkways, just as there is no sane reason for black people to be exposed to white racism or white privilege!**

Black men, as do most men, become angry and combative when they sense that their manhood has been discounted, disrespected, neglected, or not properly acknowledged. Subconsciously, many black men try to make up for or attain the manhood they seek by diminishing black women with such things as spousal abuse, date violence, sexism, assuming a tough guy or gangster persona, playing the field with many female relationships, having many babies out of wedlock, and undercutting or violating social norms. See Appendix Three for a more detailed discussion of the black man's authentic manhood profile problem.

Such worship promotes self-limiting attitudes in many black people regarding themselves, their opportunities, and their future possibilities. Fundamentalist white-male worshipping folkways teach many black people to accept the notion that God's salvation plan requires them to "bear the cross," "be humble," "to know that their place is below and behind the white man," and "to assume a victimized," or a "down and out" profile. When people internalize a belief that God has laid out a long, hard travail of suffering, victimization, and lowliness for them to follow, such a belief tends to beget behavior that will lead to self-fulfilling eventualities.

Such worship promotes alienation between black men and black women. In response to emotional sermonizing by gifted black preachers during Sunday morning worship services, many black women will ardently and openly express their love for the ancient Roman, white male idol, Jesus Christ with joyous shouts, swooning, and praises of "Dear Lord Jesus", "Just give me Jesus", "I love Lord Jesus." Meanwhile, their husbands or male companions and other black males sit quietly, watch, and listen.

From numerous observations and conversations with black men who have witnessed their wives or other black females confessing praise and love for Jesus blended with contrite appeals for Jesus to return their love, this author discerned that many of these black men experienced emotional discomfort bordering on disdain or anger toward the black female and a tinge of jealousy toward Jesus Christ. Their harboring of these negative feelings inhibits many black men from showing love, trust, openness, intimacy, and endearment toward black women. Generally, black women are intuitively aware of black men's inhibitions to express love and endearment; however they (black women) are not aware that one of the causes of these inhibitions may be that black men harbor a sullen anger and jealousy regarding the black woman's enthusiastic praises and adorations for Jesus Christ. As a result of the black man's inhibitions in showing love or endearment, black women are not inspired to present themselves (to black men) with unguarded openness, love, trust, and endearment, except as dutifulness would require, and as a consequence, a mutual alienation evolves. The black woman's feelings of alienation from the black man spur many of them (black women) to continue their tension-relieving expressions of love and adoration for Jesus Christ, and simultaneously their personal relationships and togetherness with their black male companions become even more troublesome. Generally, neither the black man nor woman recognizes that his or her alienation may have begun, in part, with the black man's jealousy of the black woman's adoration and praises of Jesus Christ, the white male Christian idol, which over several centuries has mutated into an unbeatable, superior rival to black males.

With regard to black male and female relationships, this author poses the following questions: **If people all over the world worshipped a white, blond, female as "Our Lady and Savior of the World," what would be the nature of the worshipful adorations offered during Sunday morning worship services, and how would the relationships between black men and women change?**

This author's overview of the outcomes of the black clergy's teachings:

The black community should understand that black children may be loved, fed, and cared for, but they are also mind-poisoned, beginning at an early age, by black people. **This mind-poisoning begins when black parents present, in words or pictures, the image of a white male (Jesus Christ) to their children and tell them to worship the white male imagery as their Lord and Savior.** Most likely, when these children become teen-agers, unless there is some form of intervention, they will have acquired a white superiority syndrome and will have begun to feel and think of themselves as less lovable, less beautiful, and less worthy of the better things of life than white children and lighter complexioned black children.

Black people must understand that their white-male worshipping folkways are as psychologically devastating to them as white racism. Both white racism and white male worshipping provoke feelings of low self-esteem, powerlessness, racial inferiority, psychological and cognitive dissonance, frustration, and a host of white superiority syndrome afflictions in most black people. Black people must also understand that many young black men who experience these feelings and afflictions will intuitively react with recalcitrance, anger, delinquencies, violence, and criminal behavior.

The remaining pages of this book provide supporting information/data or additional advocacy of the author's observations and conclusions regarding the negative problematic effects of white male worshipping folkways on black people.

Chapter 2

Understanding the Evolution and Content of the Nicene Creed and the Christian Trinitarian Dogma

Introduction: According to the Catholic Encyclopedia, the Trinitarian Dogma is the central doctrine of the Christian religion that expresses the truth that in the Christian Godhead there are Three Persons: the Father, the Son, and the Holy Spirit. These Three Persons being truly distinct one from another. This dogma resulted from the voting of church bishops at the Nicene Church Council in 325 CE. At this church council, the Roman emperor Constantine and the gathered church bishops composed and promulgated a document known as the Nicene Creed. The Nicene Creed was established as a tenet of faith that people must confess in order to be consider Christians. Today, in the 21st century, this Creed is regularly recited in black churches during Sunday worship services.

This author argues that the Trinitarian Dogma is grounded in the Nicene Creed and that the Creed is a superstitious myth that has little relevance or believability for intelligent people living in the 21st

century. In order to plausibly argue this point, the author presents in this chapter a review of the content, history, and believability of the Nicene Creed and the Trinitarian Dogma as described in the works and conclusions of several noted New Testament Bible scholars.

The Nicene Creed, (CE 325)

We believe in God the Father almighty,
Maker of heaven and earth
Of all that is, seen and unseen
We believe in Jesus Christ,
God's only Son, Our Lord
Who was conceived by the Holy Spirit
Born of the Virgin Mary
Suffered under Pontius Pilate
Was crucified, died, and was buried;
He descended to the dead.
On the third day he rose again;
He ascended into heaven,
He is seated at the right hand of the Father,
And he will come again to judge the living and the dead
We believe in the Holy Spirit, The holy catholic
Church, The communion of saints, The forgiveness of
sins, The resurrection of the body, And the life
everlasting. Amen.

Comments of New Testament Bible scholars:

A. Comments of Dr. Robert W. Funk, Westar institute, from his book: *Honest to Jesus*

Funk (1996) indicated that in 325 C.E., Roman emperor Constantine summoned the leaders of the church to Nicaea, a suburb of Constantinople (modern Istanbul) to adjudicate controversies among warring factions in the Christian church. Constantine presided at the council himself and saw to it that the vote was unanimous by banishing the bishops who did not put their signatures to the creed (Nicene Creed). With the Creed, there was now an official statement of correct beliefs; an orthodoxy, to which everyone had to subscribe. Those who did not, became "heretics," dissenting parties (pp. 36, 37).

Funk noted further that popular creedalism insists on a miraculous birth, accrediting miracles, death on the cross understood as a blood sacrifice, a bodily resurrection, and Jesus' eventual return to hold cosmic court and that we need only ask which of these doctrines derives from what we know of the historical Jesus. Which of them depends on Jesus' authorization or are they part of the mythological overlay invented by Jesus' early admirers employing the categories they knew and borrowed from the other religious traditions? We can no longer rest our faith on the faith of Peter or the faith of Paul.

Funk indicated further that Jesus himself is not the proper object of faith. Jesus called on his followers to trust the Father, to believe in God's domain or reign. The proper object of faith inspired by Jesus is to trust what Jesus trusted. To call for faith in Jesus is to substitute the agent for the reality, the proclaimer for the proclaimed. Jesus pointed to something he called God's domain, something he did not create; something he did not control. Funk noted that he (Funk) did not want to be misled by what Jesus' followers did: instead of looking to see what Jesus saw, his devoted disciples tended to stare at the pointing finger. If Christianity recovers its roots, it will undergo a transformation. A new version of Christianity will involve a revision of many traditional elements and the creation of new symbols, stories and a new cult. Funk stated that we must give Jesus a demotion to being a human being and not a divine. As divine son of God, co-eternal with the Father, pending cosmic judge seated at God's right hand, Jesus is insulated and isolated from his persona as the humble Galilean sage. A demoted Jesus then becomes available as the real founder of the Christian movement. With his new status, he will no longer be merely its mythical icon, embedded in the myth of the descending/ascending, dying/rising lord of the pagan mystery cults, but of one substance with us all. We need to recast Jesus in a new drama, assign him a role in a story with a different plot (pp. 304-306).

Funk noted that we need to declare the New Testament a highly uneven and biased record of various early attempts to invent Christianity. We need to reopen the question of what documents belong among the founding witnesses. In any case, said Funk, the authority of an iconic Bible is gone forever. It cannot be restored. Recognize that fact and attempt to devise a new canon of scriptures that accurately reflects the diversity in Christian origins and promotes literacy in religion (pp. 312-314).

B. Comments from reviewers of *The Five Gospels, the Search for the Authentic Words of Jesus,* a book written by the Jesus Seminar.

Introduction: The Jesus Seminar was a project of the Westar Institute, a private, nonprofit research institute devoted to improving biblical and religious literacy by making the scholarship of religion available and accessible to the general public. As part of its literacy program, the Institute sponsors seminar workshops and publications in the field of religion. At its inception in 1985, thirty scholars took up the challenge. Eventually more than 200 professionally trained specialists, called fellows, joined the group. The seminar met twice a year to debate technical papers that had been prepared and circulated in advance. At the close of debate on each agenda item, fellows of the seminar voted using colored beads to indicate the degree of authenticity of Jesus' words as recorded in the Bible. One member suggested this unofficial but helpful means of interpreting what Jesus said.

Red bead: That's Jesus!

Pink bead: Sure sounds like Jesus;

Gray bead: Well, maybe this is Jesus

Black bead: There's some mistake, this is not Jesus speaking. And according to the book jacket of the *Five Gospels,* no more than 20 percent of the sayings attributed to Jesus were uttered by him.

Three book reviews of *The Five Gospels, the Search for the Authentic Words of Jesus* are noted below.

1. "The changing face and words, of Jesus Christ," a review by Clark Morphew, (an ordained clergyman)

19

writer for the Knight-Ridder Newspapers, St. Paul (Minn.) Pioneer press (1995).

Morphew wrote in his review that according to the "Five Gospels," a new Bible published by the Jesus Seminar, that many of the sayings of Jesus were added by disciples after Jesus' death. These words were added, according to more than 100 Biblical scholars, who make up the group, to enhance the image of Jesus as a sage and miracle worker. Morphew's review stated that over the course of several years of meetings, this new translation of the Bible began to take shape. The result is a shocking assertion that most of the things Jesus is credited with saying are not authentic. For instance, the Jesus Seminar decided that Jesus never instructed his followers to pray the so-called Lord's Prayer. Now, don't panic, said Morphew, and he noted that just because a bunch of scholars says the most famous prayer in the world is not authentic does not mean we have to stop praying it. You may wonder just how these scholars know that Jesus did or did not say certain things. First they compare texts and language. They watch for cadences in speech and the use of certain words that Jesus was known to use often. For example, the only thing in the Lord's Prayer that Jesus probably said, according to the Jesus Seminar, was "Our Father." The rest of the prayer is bogus, they say.

There are other startling findings, noted Morphew. For instance, Jesus did not say, "Father, into your hands I entrust my spirit" during the crucifixion. The Jesus Seminar is not alone in telling us that there are questions about who Jesus was and his purpose in the scheme of things. This debate has been going on for decades, and it will go on a lot longer. So what will change in Christianity as the scholars contend with holy writ? For now, (1995) not much, but someday the church is going to have to face the changing identity of Jesus. Whether it will strengthen or weaken the institutional church is anybody's guess.

2. "The real meaning of Jesus," a book review appearing in the *"Bostonian Magazine," Summer 1994,* by Tertium Datur. Tertium Datur is the pen name of a Los Angeles historian (BA), classicist (MA), associate professor, and synoptic buff. Datur's review indicated that some of the Jesus Seminar decisions included the following:

Evidence that the written gospels are hearsay, or secondhand evidence; all the evangelists are reporting stories and sayings related to them by intermediate parties, none was an ear-or eyewitness to the words. The information may have passed through several parties on its way to the authors of the first written gospels, and Christian convictions eventually overwhelmed Jesus: he is made to confess what Christian had come to believe.

The fellows are convinced that Jesus did not predict his death; indeed, that he had no specific foreknowledge of it other than the premonitions a sage may have of the risk; "potential danger," in the political and cultural context.

3. Selected discussion points from this author's review of *The Five Gospels*

a. Words borrowed from the fund of common lore or the Greek scriptures are often put on the lips of Jesus (p. 22).

21

b. The evangelists frequently attribute their own statements to Jesus (p. 21).

c. The Christian community develops apologetic statements to defend its claims and sometime attributes such statements to Jesus (p. 24).

d. Jesus makes no claim to be the anointed messiah (p. 32).

C. Comments of Bishop John Shelby Spong from his book, *A New Christianity for a New World*

Spong (2002) wrote that Scripture is filled with cultural attitudes that we have long ago abandoned and with behavior that is today regarded as immoral. Concepts such the virgin birth, the physical resurrection, and the second coming are today more often regarded as symbols to be understood theologically than as events that occurred in literal history. The substitutionary view of the atonement has become grotesque, both in its understanding of a God who requires the shed blood of a human sacrifice as a prerequisite for salvation and in its definition of humanity as fallen and depraved. If these things still constitute the faith of Christian people, then Christianity has become for me and for countless others hopelessly unbelievable. Surely the essence of Christianity is not found in any or all of these propositions (pp. 2, 3).

Spong stressed that he is a Christian and has for forty-five years served the Christian church as a deacon, priest, and bishop, but he does not see Jesus as a divine. Spong notes that he does not believe:

That Jesus entered this world by the miracle of a

virgin birth or that virgin births occur anywhere except in mythology.

That the experience Christians celebrate as Easter was the physical resuscitation of the three days dead body of Jesus, or that someone literally talked with Jesus after the resurrection moment, gave him food, touched his resurrected flesh, or walked in any physical manner with his risen body. I find it interesting that all of the narratives that tell of such encounters occur only in the later gospels.

That at the end of his earthly sojourn, Jesus returned to God by ascending in any literal sense into a heaven located somewhere above the sky. My knowledge of the size of this universe reduces that concept to nonsense.

That Jesus could or did in any literal way raise the dead, overcome a medically diagnosed paralysis, restore sight to a person born blind or to one in whom the ability to see had been physiologically destroyed, banished demons, walked on water, or expanded five loaves to provide sufficient bread to feed five thousand men plus women and children (pp. 3-6).

Spong asked, "Can a person claim with integrity to be a Christian and at the same time dismiss, as he had done, so much of what has traditionally defined the content of the Christian faith?" Spong reaffirms that he is a Christian and calls the church to a radical shift from the way in which it has traditionally proclaimed its message, the way it has organized itself to broker the reservoir of spiritual power, and the way it has claimed to speak for God in human history (pp. 7-8).

D. Comments of Michael Baigent, from his book, *The Jesus Papers:*

Baigent (2006) stated that try as we might, we cannot get away from the importance of the second century A.D. for the beginning of the recording of the cult of Jesus and by the end of the century, we have hundreds of documents representing many different texts, from Gospels to various Acts (p. 76). Baigent noted that the materials used to support any of the myriad emerging viewpoints (of the Gospels) were selected by using theological criteria: someone, some group, sat down and decided from their perspective and understanding, that this book should be considered "authentic" and that book should be considered "false," that is as "orthodox" or as "heretical." The theological grounds that were used (to compose the New Testament) do not, of course, automatically justify the decisions made despite all the appeals to divine guidance that were put forth. Very human decisions were made, based upon very human priorities, mostly concerning control and power (p. 79).

According to Baigent, the books we have in our New Testament are not the only authentic traditions about Jesus. Baigent says that Roman emperor Constantine wanted unity and convened the Council of Nicaea to oppose the ideas of Arius (Bishop of Alexandria). The aim was to get support for the idea that Jesus Christ was "of one being" with God the Father, a claim that Arius and others disputed; for them, Jesus was not divine. The Council was clearly loaded against the views of Arius, but the presence of his supporters made for stormy meetings and heated discussions. In the end, a vote was taken. The exact numbers are disputed, but it is known that Arius and two of his colleagues voted against the decree; the accepted figure is that the proposition was carried by a vote of 217 to 3. Arius and his two colleagues were exiled to the Danube area. By this decision, the Council of Nicaea created the literally fantastic Jesus of faith and adopted the pretense that this was a historically accurate rendering. The Council of Nicaea produced a world of Christianity where a code of belief (the Nicene Creed) was held in common. Anything different was to be deemed heresy, to be rejected, and if possible, exterminated. We are still suffering from this today (p. 84).

By the Fifth Century A.D., the victory of the Jesus of faith over the Jesus of history was, in all practical matters, complete. The myth that the two are the same became theologically justified and as such an accepted truth. However, the protectors of orthodoxy ruthlessly protected the faith by doing to other Christians what the pagan emperors had done previously. In A.D. 386 the Church executed Priscillian, bishop of Avila, on the grounds of heresy. This was the first execution ordered by the Church in order to defend its position. All roads may have led to Rome, but over the succeeding centuries, so did an increasing number of rivulets of blood. The price of theological unity was paid not just in gold, but in lives as well (p. 89).

E. Comments from the *Holy Bible* (*KJV*): The ancient Roman Christian Church allowed the following writings to be a part of the New Testament of the Holy

Bible:

Luke: 18:19. "And Jesus said unto him, Why callest thou me good: None is good, save one, that is, God."

Matt: 15:9. "But in vain they do worship me, teaching for doctrine the commandments of men."

Mark 12:29. "And Jesus answered him, 'the first of all the commandments is Hear, O Israel, the Lord our God is one Lord . . .'"

This author argues that these Biblical citations attributed to Prophet Jesus infer that Jesus is not God and should not be worshipped, and as such these citations appear to refute the assertions made in the Nicene Creed and the Trinitarian Dogma.

F. Comments of Professor Bart D. Ehrman from his book, *Lost Christianities:*

Ehrman (2003) noted that during the 1st and 2nd centuries there were wide diversities in the forms of Christianity and beliefs embraced by people who understood themselves to be follower of Jesus. This diversity was possible because there was no New Testament. The books that now make up the New Testament had been written by the end of the 1st century, but there were many other books (gospels) written as well that were not included in what we now know as the New Testament, although some of these gospels were written by early apostles of Jesus. These books are referred to as "Lost Scriptures." Some one decided that only four of these gospels and not others should be acceptable as part of the New Testament and what form of Christianity was acceptable and "right" and what forms were "heretical" teachings or false ideas. This victorious party rewrote the history of the scripture controversies claiming that its own view had always been the majority view of Christians and gained itself political power. If some other form of Christianity had won the early struggle for political dominance, the Doctrine of the Trinity might never have developed (pp. 23-26).

Erhman (2004) indicated in his *Lecture 23 on the Doctrine of the Trinity (Part 2)* that the doctrine of the Trinity does not appear to have been pronounced by Jesus, Paul, or any other Christian writers during the first hundred years or so of Christianity, and cannot be found explicitly stated in the earliest Christian writings. The only passage of the New Testament that declared the doctrine (1John 5:7-8) was not originally a part of the text, but was added by doctrinally astute scribes at a later date. It was not found in any Greek manuscripts until the 11th century (p. 43).

G. Comments of Professor Gerd Ludemann, from his book, *The Resurrection of Christ; a Historical Inquiry:*

Ludemann (2004) wrote that although early Christian faith confesses the resurrection and the church is built on it, historical research shows with definite clarity that Jesus was not raised from the dead. The insistence by Paul and early Christian faith generally on the "fact" of Jesus' resurrection by God must now be regarded as a falsification. Therefore unless we totally re-define the word, people can no longer justify calling themselves Christians. For two thousand years an abiding faith in Jesus' resurrection has displayed enormous power, but because of its utter groundlessness we must now acknowledge that it has all along been a world wide historical hoax (p. 190). Ludemann indicated that because the resurrection is so doubtful and can no longer serve as a basis for our lives, he chooses to live in a house built on a solid foundation rather than in a priestly domicile suspended in the sky. Ludemann indicated that if we take seriously the nature of historical knowledge and our own human dignity, we cannot be Christian any longer (by the old definition). Since Jesus did not rise from the dead, those who nonetheless continue to claim that obsolete title of "Christian" are deceiving themselves (p. 205).

Summary of Bible scholars' comments:

The opinions and conclusions of the Biblical scholars we have cited suggest that the Nicene Creed and the Trinitarian Doctrine are composed of myths and superstitions that are no longer plausible or relevant for educated people living in the 21st century. These scholars seem to agree that over sixteen hundred years ago, there were many versions of Christianity and that at the Nicene Council, with the concurrence of Roman emperor Constantine, the Roman Catholic Church promulgated the Nicene Creed and thus formalized and stabilized Christianity. Soon thereafter, the Roman Catholic Church began enforcing the Creed and the Dogma by torture, death, and the threat of death.

"Kissing the Face of God"

Figure Two

Chapter 3

Christian Worship and Black Inferiority: comments from Black Psychologists, Sociologists, and Educators

Introduction: The author presents in this chapter comments of selected black psychologists, sociologists, educators, and other black professionals regarding their assessment of the effects of white male worshipping folkways on black people's thinking and self-perceptions.

A. Comments of Arthur (Last name unknown) an attendee at a Slave Descendent Freedom Seminar and Conference on June 18, 2006, in Laurel, Maryland. Arthur is a mature, educated black man from Eastern Maryland. During one section of the seminar that dealt with religion, Arthur spoke the following words with frustration and an authoritative tone, "I know in my heart that can't no virgin have a baby, but I'm going to be Christian until I die." (Most of the seminar participants laughed and so did Arthur.) **This author's reaction to Arthur's comments**: Arthur's statement gives voice to his intellect and to his faith in Christian ethics and morals at the same time.

Arthur answers the question, "Can a person be a follower of Jesus' teachings or philosophy without the trappings of the superstitious myths and the false faith tales mandated by Constantine-certified Christianity?" Arthur's answer is "yes," but he is clearly experiencing psychological dissonance between what he believes and what he is suppose to believe as a Christian.

B. Comments of Dr. Na'im Akbar from his book; *Breaking the Chains of Psychological Slavery.*

Akbar (1991) states that we must seek to overcome the plantation ghost by identifying the forces which lead to enslavement and self-abasement. We must avoid the psychologically destructive representation of God in a Caucasian form (p. 11).

Akbar noted further that the seriousness of the Caucasian religion imagery is revealed by the realization of the absence of concern about these images. Almost no one deals with the representation of God and the entire heavenly host in Caucasian flesh. Perhaps the most disturbing fact is that this Caucasian image of divinity has become an unconsciously controlling factor in the psychology of African Americans. After 100 years, Akbar noted, we (black people) still govern none of the institutional forces that affect our lives. There is no successful, independent black institution that is independent both in thought and economic control of white ideas and institutions. Unfortunately, we often do not care that we don't control anything and furthermore, we are defiant in preserving our dependence. One of the persisting difficulties facing African American people is the difficulty of thinking independently. Black people are constrained by the perception that creativity and innovation are the exclusive privilege of those who are similar to the image of the Divinity (pp. 58-61).

C. Comments of Dr. Amos Wilson from the introduction of his book; *Black on Black Violence.* Wilson (1990) indicated that the causal factor in Black criminality and violence is White Supremacy. The violently oppressed react violently to their oppression. When their reactionary violence cannot be effectively directed at their oppressor or effectively applied to their self-liberation, it then will be directed and applied destructively to themselves. Black men kill each other because they have not yet chosen to challenge and neutralize on every front the widespread power of white men to rule over their lives. Wilson indicated that black on black criminality and violence represent quests for power and outraged protest against a sense of powerlessness and insignificance and that the demise of black on black violence will begin with the renaissance of authentic black power. When we speak of African-American/Pan-African self-empowerment, we refer not to the bogus, illusory power of token black house-servants, the mock White power of the Black bourgeoisies, or the sycophantic, boot licking power of the black politicians. Wilson stated that we neither include the pie-in-the-sky, White God fearing power of black preachers, or the oleaginous diplomatic power of puppet, neocolonial African "heads of state." Wilson spoke of a true and honest African American/Pan-African Power which springs full-force from African manhood, womanhood, and humanity: a power which harnesses the abundant intellectual, emotional, behavioral, cultural, spiritual and material resources of African peoples and uses them to secure and protect the survival, well-being, and self actualization of the total African community.

This author's reaction to Dr. Wilson's comments: Dr. Wilson speaks of black violence as a reaction against the oppressive effects of white supremacy. This author argues that the black community's white-male worshipping folkways is one of the most effective tools of white supremacy because it subliminally attacks the mind and spirit of black people, especially young black men, and renders the same oppression on black people's minds as does white racism.

D.   Comments of Dr. Francis Welsing from her book; *The Isis Papers and the Secret of the Colors.* Welsing (1991) tells us that absolutely critical to the white supremacy system of religious thought was the formation of the image of a white man as the son of God.   Because the brain-computer functions most fundamentally on logic circuits at deep unconscious levels, it automatically computes that God the father is also a white male. If God is other than white, he would have produced a black (or other non-white) son. Welsing stated that any person programmed to accept the Christian religion, whether conscious of it or not, has the image and concept of God as a white man in the logic network of his/her brain-computer, and with this unconscious logic circuit of "God is a white man" firmly in place, white domination over non-white people could last for one trillion years. Welsing reiterated that all black and other non-white people who profess to be members of the Christian (white supremacy) religion, whether they are conscious of it or not, worship the white man as God (not as "a" god, but as "the" God), and that in the unconscious logic networks of their individual brain-computer lies the logic that the white man is the supreme or ultimate reality, the Being perfect in power, wisdom, and goodness, whom men worship as creator and ruler of the universe. Welsing emphasized that as a general and child psychiatrist, she is fully aware of the destruction spawned by the unconscious logic implant that "God is a white man." However, no matter what the level of initial trauma felt when this logic circuit is brought to conscious awareness, it must come fully to light and be yanked out. Indeed, there can be no mental health, self-respect or positive self-concept for black or other non-white peoples as long as this specious and destructive logic circuit remains in place. To be black and accept consciously or unconsciously the image of God as a white man is the highest possible form of self-negation and lack of self-respect under the specific conditions of white domination. Such perception, emotional response, and thought are therefore insane. This logic circuit ensures that Black people always will look up to white people and, therefore down upon themselves. Only by breaking this logic circuit, can the concept of black and non-white liberation become a reality. This is the direction in which we blacks must propel ourselves as we enter the 21st century (pp. 163-172).

E. Comments of Dr. Jawanza Kunjufu from his book, *"Adam! Where are you?" Why most Black Men Don't Go to church.* Kunjufu (1994) wrote of how the brothers discussed that they had a problem with the white, blonde, blue eyed image of Jesus proudly displayed in the church sanctuary. According to Kunjufu, one brother said, "I will go to church when that lying image comes down. I'm not worshiping no white man." Another brother said that when he mentioned the image (of Jesus Christ) to his wife, she said "What differences does it make? We need to worship Him in spirit and in truth." Then I just looked at her and realized how deep the self-hatred is and that the legacy of slavery remains. She didn't see the contradiction in keeping a white, blonde, blue-eyed image, while saying we need to worship Him in spirit and in Truth (pp. 60, 61).

This author's reaction to Dr. Kunjufu comments: Dr. Kunjufu touched the surface of the issue regarding presenting the image of a white male as the savior of the world to black men. This author agrees that such images should be removed from the picture windows and walls of church sanctuaries, but the problem goes deeper than a picture on a wall or in the stained glass windows of churches. This author argues that such images must be removed from black people's minds! Such pictures and icons (of white divinities in black churches) represent the way black people think. Most black people have accepted, in their heart of hearts, the image of a white male as God, the supreme force and source of power. If this were not the case, images of

35

white divinities in black churches would have been removed long ago. If black people are to gain their psychological freedom from white superiority syndrome afflictions, they must remove the white-male worshipping icons, pictures and murals from their minds and their churches with a straight-forward and purposeful image-removal program.

F. Comments in a letter (Sept '08) from a retired black educator (who wishes to remain anonymous) who worked in the Fairfax County, Virginia, Public Schools system. ". . . black and white American preachers are responsible for the alarming growth of wide spread ignorance. This devastating result derives from the fact that the so-called "faithful" refuse to read scientific non-fiction which reveals the nature of all things, and they refuse to go beyond the tiny, harmful knowledge that their ancestors possessed. . . . It is totally unrealistic that a very pale, male Caucasian would have been born a semi-god that close to North Africa, but they cling to this concept. Then there is information readily available which highlights the facts that a Christian semi-god, Jesus Christ, occurred at a time when other ancient cultures had abandoned the concepts of miraculous births and human resurrections. Just turn to Kersey Graves' *The World's Sixteen Crucified Saviors*, or John G. Jackson's *Christianity Before Christ*, or Gary Greenberg's *Bible Myths: the African Origins of the Jewish People*, and others to see how the ancient Hebrews plagiarized sources from other cultures for their stories of miracles and resurrections. . . . Man invented institutions and the books to sustain them, such as "holy books" and rituals. Europeans under Constantine bound together a white bible which demanded the allegiance of everyone in the new Roman Empire. Don't ever expect them to abolish or abandon their image of a white god and his semi-god son, Jesus, because these images hold together a holy empire whose monetary value and worth has to be in the trillions of dollars. All that counts is the money flow and they know that whites have a greater abundance of cash assets than non-whites. Not that it can be done, but I believe that anyone who is powerful enough to influence the abolition of these white icons will be assassinated by order of holy men from high above."

Sincerely,

/s/

G. Comments of Dr. Carter G. Woodson from his book; *The Mis-education of the Negro.* Woodson (1933) asserted that in the church the Negro has had sufficient freedom to develop this institution in his own way, but he has failed to do so. His religion is merely a loan from whites who have enslaved and segregated the Negro. The dominant thought is to make use of the dogma of the whites as a means to an end. In chameleon-like fashion, the Negro has taken up almost everything religious which has come along instead of thinking for himself. The Negro has borrowed the ideas of his traducers instead of delving into things and working out thoughts of his own. Some Negro leaders know better, but they hold their following by keeping the people divided, in emphasizing nonessentials, the insignificance of which the average man may not appreciate (pp. 57-61). **Woodson stated further that instead of accepting and trying to carry out the theories which the exploiters of humanity have brought them for a religious program, the Negroes should forget their differences and in the strength of a united church bring out a new interpretation of Christ to this unwilling world.** Following the religious teachings of their traducers, Negroes do not show any more common sense than a people would in permitting criminals to enact the laws and establish the procedures of the courts by which they are to be tried (p. 147).

H. Excerpts of a Letter, (May 18, 1998), from Dr. Wendell A. Jean-Pierre, Sr., retired educator. "Dr. Bell, the abstract of your paper indicates that your presentation (see note below) merits consideration, but you have your work cut out for you, trying to detoxify African-descended peoples in the U.S. from the shackles of the Christian religion, which was initially imbedded in them to rob them of their militancy. The priests, missionaries, etc, were the spiritual avant-garde police in Africa and subsequently in the U.S. to condition the thought structure of colonized people (non-whites mainly), so that they would react like Pavlov's dogs. But I guess the struggle must be waged on all levels. And if your adversary is too strong to overthrow frontally, a cluster of forces must nibble away at him unceasingly. Your emphasis on the "Trinitarian belief system" falls within the ambient of one of the approaches to hasten the demise of a virulent racism that locates its origins in all of the institutions of this country. . . . Your point that Black people "must learn to worship only God," seems to be a viable alternative. Although, I sometimes succumb to the proposition that if there is a god, it is no friend of our race. My advice to you in getting your message out, is that you contact the various chairs of Afro-American Departments through out the U.S. and see if there would be any interest in their inviting you to their various campuses to address the students. But you would have to adapt your lecture to students and not to the professors as you have done in your presentation."

Sincerely,
/s/ Dr. Wendell A. Jean-Pierre, Sr.

Referenced Presentation: "Christian Trinitarianism: A Psychogenic catalyst of Racism and Low Black Achievement," by. Christopher C. Bell Jr., Ed.D. given at the African Heritage Studies Association (AHSA), 30th Annual Conference, March 26-29, 1998, Radisson Hotel, New Orleans, Louisiana.

I. Excerpts of a letter (March 2006), from Nana Dr. Kofi Abayie Kokroko, historian. Every religion incorporates the customs and traditions of the founder of that religion. Caucasians do not have a cultural problem with Christianity, but Africans have a leviathan problem because Christianity has destroyed any semblance of African culture. Christianity in Africa has demolished African self-esteem by practicing the superiority of Christianity. For example, in Ghana, a birth certificate requires a person to first list his Christian name regardless of whether or not he is a Christian. Christian names must be put before one's ethnic name. That little gesture says a Christian name is superior to one's ethnic name. When I meet a Ghanaian the first time, over 90 percent of them will give me their Christian name. When I ask what day of the week were you born, many have forgotten. In Ghanaian culture, after the third day, a baby is given the name of the day he was born. I was born on Friday, thus my first name is Kofi.

There are numerous examples that I could give whereby Christianity has demolished African culture, but the most insidious, orchestrated act that Christianity has done is to assume Africans, the first people to have civilization and religion, need to be taught religion. Even more detrimental, many Africans have been convinced, by Christian missionaries, that if they want to save their souls, they must learn about God from Christians.

Sincerely,
/s/ Nana

Summary of comments from the cited black psychologists, sociologists, and educators: The commentators in this chapter appear to agree that in America's white supremacy culture there can be no positive collective self-concept for black people as long as they worship with the rationale that God in one form or other is a white male. Thus, as long as black

40

people maintain their white-male worshipping folkways, they will never free themselves from white superiority syndrome afflictions, and will never be able to think of themselves as equal to white people. These same worshipping, believing, and self-assessing phenomena are at work in Africa just as they are in America.

Chapter 4

How Black Churches contribute to the "gap" in Academic Achievement between Black and White High School Students

Prologue: The substance of this essay was delivered as an oral presentation at the Alumni of Color Conference (AOCC), March 5-7, 2004, at Harvard University Graduate School of Education by Dr. Christopher C. Bell Jr., CAS'75.

Presentation

Introduction: I wish to thank the sponsors and alumni for the opportunity to make this presentation, which is entitled, How Black Churches contribute to the "gap" in academic achievement between black and white high school students. The "gap" refers to the differences in the academic achievement testing results of black high school students as compared to the higher academic achievement testing results of their white counterparts.

Several educational researchers: Blau, Jensen, Jenks,

Ogbu, Herrenstein and Murray, and Mostella have attempted to explain the "why" in the difference between the academic achievement testing results of black and white high school children. These researchers indicated that their findings suggest that the gap is a manifestation of differences in white children and black children IQ's or differences in social/economic learning situations that are disadvantageous to black students, or a combination of both of these factors. In addition, these researchers concluded that black teenagers as a group exhibited more signs of low self-esteem and ego-deficiencies as compared to their white counterparts. However, these researchers rarely mentioned the causes or events that produced or promoted the low self-esteem or ego-deficiencies in the black students whom they had observed.

My analyses of the findings of these researchers, my observations and studies of school and classroom learning situations of black children, and my observations and investigations of black children's learning environments that extend beyond the formal school setting suggest that a key factor that impacts negatively on the psyche of black children is their belief structure. My analyses suggest that many adolescent black children have acquired a set of beliefs which afflicts them with what I refer to as a White Superiority Syndrome (WSS). It is this syndrome that accounts for much of their mental and emotional dispositions, attitudes, personal behavior, self-esteem, and future outlook.

Definition and scope of the white superiority syndrome:

The White Superiority Syndrome (WSS) is the belief of many black and white people that white people, as a group, are "better" and "smarter" and "more beautiful" than black people, and thus white people are more deserving of the good things of life.

In America, by the time they are teenagers, most black and white children are aware of America's white superiority philosophy. Most black and white people subliminally develop the White Superiority Syndrome (WSS) as a result of their normal, unassuming alignment of their thinking and actions with the customs and expectations of the white superiority philosophy of America's culture. Unless the black or white child experiences some intervention by way of actions or circumstances or mentoring, he will generally acquire the WSS. Nobody directly "tells or teaches" the black child that he is inferior to white people, and nobody directly "tells or teaches" the white child that he is superior to black people. Most people subliminally acquire the WSS is a result of their normal functioning in their social and cultural environments where America's accepted preferences and valuing prevails.

The problem with the WSS is that it affects white children differently than it does black children. The WSS provides white adolescents with an emotional and psychic foundation of comfort and control, but it inflicts emotional stress, psychological dissonance, and a sense of inferiority on black adolescents. The WSS also engenders a color caste mentality that (1) infuses in

44

many black people a sense of being a member of a "low caste" group because of their dark skin color, and mediates downward black children's motivations and impulses to compete with white children in intellectual and educational pursuits or competencies, and (2) infuses in many white people a sense of being a member of a "high caste" group because of their white skin and promotes in white children an urge to "do better" than black children in intellectual and educational competencies.

The black church and the white superiority syndrome

I argue that the teachings and beliefs espoused in the worship services by the black clergy in black churches are factors that promote and instill the white superiority syndrome within the black community and into the minds of black children. What are these teachings and beliefs? My argument is based on the following hypotheses.

First hypothesis: That the black church espouses the following Christian theological cluster of beliefs that promotes the acquisition of a white superiority syndrome by many black adolescents:

a. That God begot a Son named Jesus Christ who is divine and worthy of worship, (and depicted as a white male);

b. That Mary, Jesus' mother is the Mother of God;

c. That salvation of the soul is only possible by acknowledging belief in Jesus Christ, a White male.

Second hypothesis: That in many black children a white superiority syndrome promotes low self-esteem,

45

emotional dissonance, an inferiority complex, and mediates downward their motivations and impulses to compete with white children in intellectual and educational pursuits or competencies. The gap in the academic achievement testing results of black and white adolescents is, in part, a manifestation of the effects of the white superiority syndrome on black adolescents.

Third hypothesis: That the academic achievement gap will continue with little change until the deleterious and disabling beliefs cited above have been dismantled or neutralized.

Discussion: Before we can clearly show the deleterious effects of the Christian theological belief structure on the black adolescent's psyche, we must speak to several related issues: (1) the importance of belief, and (2) understanding human motivation.

1. The importance of belief:

According to Murphy (1963), what children believe about themselves, about their world, and about their future adult role in the world mediates how they will perform inside and outside of school. Generally, what people believe determines their attitudes. Our attitudes are inseparable from our beliefs; and further, it is our attitudes that direct our everyday choices of actions and reactions to the outside world **and to the world within**. Beliefs may be benignant or malignant to the believer. Nevertheless, the believer's actions and attitudes will flow endlessly from the reservoir of the variety and intensity of his belief system. In short, our actions are grounded in our attitudes and our attitudes are grounded in our beliefs (pp. 23-30).

Fishbein and Ajzeen, (1975) explained that beliefs are the fundamental building blocks in our conceptual structure. On the basis of direct observation or information received from outside sources or by way of various inferences and processes, a person learns or forms a number of beliefs about an object. He associates the object with various attributes. In this manner, he forms beliefs about himself, about other people, about institutions, and behavioral events. The totality of a person's beliefs serves as the informational base that ultimately determines his attitudes, intentions, and behavior (p. 13).

2. Understanding human motivation:

The scholars, Sickles (1976), Raynor and Entin (1982) tell us that motivations are the inner needs and drives (motives) of individuals, and that the intensity of our motives is determined as much by our self-systems (sense of who we are or how we visualized our future selves) as it is by the requirements placed on us by the behavioral system (outside authority requirements). Motivations that spring from the self-system are referred to as internal motivations and those motives that are placed on us by the behavioral system (outside authority requirements) are referred to as external motivation.

Sergiovanni and Starratt (1971) assert that whether Johnny learns X or not depends largely upon how Johnny feels about learning X. Johnny's learning of X or of anything else is largely affected by his concept of self, his levels of aspiration, his unique motivational orientation, the perceived relevancy to his need structure of what is being offered for learning, his level of commitment, his previous experience with similar learning situations, his level of maturation, his value-belief system, and his interpersonal entanglements and commitments to others (p. 127).

Discussion of the beliefs that promote the white superiority syndrome:

Belief 1: That God, the Creator of the world, has a begotten Son, Jesus, who is divine and is historically depicted as a white male humanoid and is worthy of the worship of black adolescents.

Comments by Dr. Francis Welsing, a prominent black psychologist: Welsing (1991) notes that absolutely critical to the White Supremacy System of religious thought was the formation of the image of a white male as the Son of God. This white male image is referred to as Christ. ... Because the brain computer (the mind) functions most fundamentally on logic circuits at deep unconscious levels, it automatically computes that God the father is also a white male. With this unconscious logic circuit of "God is a white man" firmly in place, white domination over non-white people could last for one trillion years (p.166). Welsing goes on to say that to be black and accept consciously or unconsciously the image of God as a white man is the highest possible form of self-negation and lack of self-respect under the specific conditions of white domination. Such perception, emotional response and thought are therefore insane and such logic ensures that black people always will look up to white people and therefore down upon themselves. Only by breaking that logic circuit can the concept of black and other non-white liberation become a reality (p. 172).

Comments by Na'im Akbar, a Professor of Clinical Psychology: Akbar (1991) tells us that in Judeo-Christian imagery, the Caucasian bows down and worships himself and the African American (bows down) worships the Caucasian as a God as well. Akbar states that the most obvious problem that comes from the experience of seeing God in an image of somebody other than yourself is that it creates an idea that that image, that person, is superior and you are inferior. Once you have a concept that begins to make you believe that you are not as good as other people, your actions follow you mind. . . . So if you have internalized the view of a deity and a creator as being in flesh, having a nationality and physical characteristics different from yourself, then you automatically assume that you are inferior in your own characteristics. . . . You begin to believe that you have less human potential than those who look like the image (p. 48).

Comments from the National Association of Black Psychologists: Black psychologists have acknowledged the negativism that the white male God image has on the psyche of black children. The National Convention of the Association of Black Psychologists in Cherry Hill, New Jersey, August 13-16, 1980, approved the following resolution.
Whereas: . . . We recognize the portrayal of the Divine as Caucasian as the most pervasive assertion of white supremacy . . .

Whereas: the portrayal of the Divine in images of Caucasian flesh constitutes an oppressive instrument, destructive to the self-esteem of black people throughout the world and is directly destructive to the psychological well-being of black children.

Resolve: That the Association recommends the removal of Caucasoid images of the Divinity from public display and from places of worship; . . . and that copies of this resolution be provided to national religious bodies, national civil rights organizations, and to select religious leaders, for the purpose of opening up an educational dialogue for change."

Summary of comments:

Belief 1: The belief that God begot a Son named "Jesus Christ" who is depicted as a white male and worthy of worship infers to the black adolescent that God is white.

Comment: Such a belief on the part of black children will poison their minds with a sense of racial inferiority and instill in them a white superiority syndrome. This belief promotes a "god image" in the likeness of their white classmates who are now their academic competitors. Silently and without fanfare, this belief leads black adolescents, especially black males, to a diminished and impoverished self-hood and often to a sullen anger toward their white schoolmates and their black communities. This belief also promotes deep psychological dissonance and a lack of motivation to compete in those things that blacks have come to believe that whites have reserved for themselves, such as academics, and a gap in academic achievement testing naturally follows. The black adolescent knows that academics for whites lead to high paying positions, political control, and wealth, but such is not true for blacks.

Is it reasonable to expect most black youth to be motivated toward competitive academics with their white classmates when their church tells them via creeds, sermons, and pictures that their God, their Lord and Savior looks like and shares the genetic traits of their white classmates? Can one expect black adolescents to be motivated to do their best when their survey of what counts and who counts alerts them that God has already willed the future adult, first-class positions to their white classmates, who look like God and who share God's genetic traits?

Belief 2: That Mary, the mother of Jesus Christ, is the Mother of God. This belief is often accompanied by a picture of Mary and Baby Jesus which is referred to as "Madonna and Child" and presented to black children as God and his mother.

Comment: I argue that for young black children, the white Madonna-Child portrayal representing God and his mother has become a symbolic icon. The introduction of this icon to black children is probably the start of their first baby-steps toward self-rejection and toward embracing whiteness as being superior, more beautiful, and more God-like than their own brown-ness or blackness. Although young black children may not be old enough to understand the socio-religious implication of the Madonna and Child

51

picture, black adolescents with their newly acquired "formal operational thinking" will be able to discern that the picture looks like their white classmates and their mothers. And thus, inside the psyche of black adolescents begins the quiet, deep, psychological negative-ness toward their non-white skin coloring and features.

I argue that with their declining sense of themselves and their increasing sense of the uselessness for them of high academic achievement, black adolescents will not put forth their best efforts toward academic achievement, and this lack of motivation contributes to the gap between black and white adolescents in academic achievement testing.

Imam W.D. Mohammed (Muslim Journal Newspaper) offers up the following question that is worth pondering: **What would happen if all people would sit in churches throughout the world for centuries, with the image of an African-American man as Savior of the world before them? What would this do to the minds of the world's children?**

Belief 3: That salvation (entry into paradise or heaven) of the soul in the life-after-death is attainable with a simple confession of belief in Jesus Christ as Lord and Savior.

Comment: I argue that this belief places little or no value on personal excellence, hard work, self-discipline, and good behavior in this world as a means of attaining a heavenly after-life. Thus, this belief nullifies and is counter-productive to personal obligations of maintaining high moral principles, valuing the importance of honest work, striving to be successful or studying to make good grades in school. This belief subliminally devalues academic achievement motivation as a desirable model of social behavior. With regard to black adolescents, this belief becomes an academic achievement de-motivator and thus also contributes to the gap in the academic achievement testing scores between black and white adolescents.

Actions Recommended to be taken by the black church regarding the above beliefs/creeds:

Black church authorities, black psychologists, black sociologists, and Bible scholars should meet and confer with the intent of promoting changes that will eliminate the creeds and teachings cited above. Specifically, I recommend these professionals take the following actions:

Remove images of so-called divine characters and icons from all areas of worship, school areas, and offices. I contend that the God of Creation is too great to be captured on paper or in stone and is beyond the imagination of men.

Demote Jesus Christ from the theological, creedal status of a divinity and recognize Prophet Jesus as a man, a human being who was a gifted teacher and healer. This deconstruction of the idol Jesus Christ and reconstruction of Prophet Jesus as a human being should be accompanied with teachings that explain the origin and history of the adoption of this Son of God creed by early church authorities. It should be noted that this creed has already undergone scholarly scrutiny that has intellectually and theologically severely challenged its integrity.

Promote a "new" Christianity grounded in values and principles related to the just, equitable, and compassionate relations between human beings that are not dependent on supernaturalism or miracle stories. To do this, black clergy and church authorities must re-educate themselves about the history of Christianity, including the political and theological arguments leading up to the acceptance of the Nicene Creed and the promulgation of the Trinitarian Dogma.

Continue community uplift and character building related activities, but formalize the "God-talk" and rituals with a pedagogy that acknowledges only the "God of the Creation" as divine and worthy of worship.

What if?

What if the concerted efforts of the black clergy, black church authorities, black sociologists, black psychologists and Bible scholars fail to dismantle or eliminate these creeds/beliefs? I argue that if these black professionals fail to meet, confer, and eliminate these creeds (Dogma), we can expect:

1. Black adolescents' academic achievement relative to their white cohorts will not improve in any significant way, regardless of how much money is added for education, or the high skill-level of teachers, or the comfort of the learning environment.

2. Black adolescents will continue to leave for school each day mentally and emotionally unable to compete at their best with their white classmates regarding academic achievement.

3. Black people as a group will never gain a true sense of mental and psychological liberation and in their heart of hearts will forever feel inferior to white people.

This author is in agreement with Salley and Behrn (1988) who stated that the tragedy of the black experience in relation to Christianity is that Christianity was and is unable to provide blacks with the necessary ability to free them from white oppression and a sense of inferiority (pp. 65-71).

Long ago, Dr. Carter G. Woodson (1933) noted that in the church, the Negro has borrowed the ideas of his traducers instead of delving into things and working out thoughts of his own. Woodson asserted that while serving as the avenue of the oppressor's propaganda, the Negro Church, although doing some good, has prevented the union of diverse elements and has kept the race too weak to overcome foes who have purposely taught Negroes how to quarrel and fight about trifles (pp. 57-61).

So today, I challenge the 21st century black clergy, black psychologists, black sociologists and Bible scholars to meet and confer for the purpose of dismantling the white male god image and the accompanying theological creeds and beliefs. As a minimum these black professionals must combine their talents and efforts to write, stage, and act out an uplifting, inspiring, spiritual agenda of a "new" Christianity that is not structured on belief in a "personality" as their God or on superstitions and miracles. If these black professionals can meet this challenge, and they can, black people will be able to learn to love themselves, and black adolescents will become emotionally able to compete vigorously and favorably in all areas and levels of human endeavors with any other ethnic group.

Thank you for the opportunity to make this presentation.

Epilogue

The gathering of 15 to 20 alumni who heard this presentation responded with a mixture of surprise, anxiety, and inquisitiveness. An extended question and answer period followed and revolved around my recommendation that Jesus Christ be demoted from "god status" to "prophet status," and be thought of as a human being. I've noted below some of the questions and answers that followed the presentation.

Q: You talk about demoting Jesus Christ to a human being, but doesn't the Gospel of John say that Jesus is "the way, the truth, and the light?"

A. I cited Jesus' own statements (Mark 12:29; Mark 18:19; Matt 19:16 and 17) and explained the time span between the writings of John and the death of Jesus and the probable politics at work when the gospel of John was written. I also pointed out that such claims of Jesus' divinity weren't present in the earliest Gospels.

Q: Why not have a black Jesus? Wouldn't that solve the problem?

A: I said this would be less sensible than utilizing a white Jesus. What black child or white child upon entering puberty and learning about the world would be naive enough to think that the Lord and Savior of the whole world was black? Further, it is folly to worship any human personality.

Q: I need to see some numbers about the relationships between Catholics and Protestants and church goers versus non-church goers and their individual grades before I can accept even the black psychologists' resolution.

A: I don't have such numbers, but do you acknowledge the phenomenon I referred to as the "White Superiority Syndrome?" (Response) Yes, that much makes sense.

Q: I'm a Sunday school teacher, and I don't see a sense of low self-esteem among my children. How do you account for this?

A: How old are the children in your class? (Response): They are eight to eleven years old.

(My response): I suggest that we give them a few more years to mature into teenagers and then take a close look.

Q: Dr. Bell, have you read the writings of Dr. Amos Wilson? (Response: No, I have not). **Questioner:** I suggest you read his writings. (**Response:** Thanks)

Q: I reluctantly admit that this White Superiority Syndrome is a problem, but what are the best means for disrupting or intervening in its effects?

A: I have not studied in detail the various overall means and methods that might be possible. However my presentation only dealt with the influence of the black church in afflicting black people with a white superiority syndrome. There are many other realities about living in America that afflict black people with this syndrome, but my presentation and recommendations are directed at the black church because the black church is an area that black people control. So I've limited my discussion to the elimination or neutralization of the white superiority syndrome that starts in the black church. However, it is my belief that if we can start there and be successful, we can be successful in eliminating the White Superiority Syndrome across a broad span of America's society.

None of this will be easy, but it must be done if black people are to gain psychological liberation from the White Superiority Syndrome and truly open themselves to the real possibility of becoming the best people they can become.

Q: So, Dr. Bell, what's your religion?
A: I fellowship with Unitarian Universalists.

Q: Who and what are Unitarian Universalists?
A: That's another presentation and it's beyond my planned intentions, but let's talk over coffee.

References

Akbar, Na'im. Chains and Images of Psychological Slavery. Jersey City, NJ: New Mind Productions, 1991

Bell, Christopher. The Belief Factor and the White Superiority Syndrome. Bloomington, IN: 1St Books Library, 2001

Blau, Zena Smith. Black Children/White Children, Competence, Socialization and Social Structure. New York, NY: The Free Press, 1981

Branden, Nathaniel. The Six Pillars of Self-Esteem. New York, NY: A Bantam Book, 1994

Erickson, Eric. Identity, Youth and Crisis. New York, NY: W.W. Norton, 1968

Fishbein, Martin & Icek, Ajzen. Belief, Attitude, Intention and Behavior, Reading, MA: Addison-Wesley, 1975

Goodman, M. Race Awareness in Young Children. Reading, MA: Addison-Wesley, 1964

Herrenstein, R. & Murray, C. The Bell Curve. New York, NY: The Free Press, 1994

Jenks, Christopher. Inequality: A reassessment of the effect of Family and Schooling in America. New York,

NY: Harper and Row, 1972

Jensen, Arthur. "How Much Can We Boost IQ and Scholastic Achievement?" Harvard Educational Review. Cambridge, MA: Harvard University Press, 1969

Mostella, F. & Moynihan, D. On the Equality of Educational Opportunity. New York, NY: Vintage Books, 1972

Ogbu, John. Minority Education and Caste. New York, NY: Academic Press, 1978

Piaget, Jean. The Growth of Logical Thinking from Childhood to Adolescence. New York, NY: Basic Books, 1958

Porter, JDR. Black Child, White Child. Cambridge, MA: Harvard University Press, 1971

Raynor, Joel O. & Entin, E.I. Motivation, Career Striving and Aging. Washington, DC: Hemisphere Publishing Corporation, 1982

Sickles, William R. Psychology: A Matter of Mind. Dubuque, IA: Kendall/Hunt Publishing Company, 1976

Sergiovanni, Thomas & Starratt, Robert. Emerging Patterns of Supervision: Human Perspectives, New York, NY: McGraw-Hill Book Company, 1971

Welsing, Francis. <u>The Isis Paper; Keys to the Colors</u>. Chicago, Ill: The Third World Press, 1991

Woodson, Carter G. <u>The Mis-education of the Negro.</u> Washington, DC: The Associate Publishers Inc., 1933

"TO TELL YOU THE TRUTH, WE DON'T KNOW EXACTLY.
BUT IF YOU UNDERSTAND
THAT THIS IS GOD'S ONLY BEGOTTEN SON,
YOU NOW HAVE AN IDEA OF WHAT GOD LOOKS LIKE."

Figure Three

Chapter 5

The Original Petition

Introduction:

On July 20, 2006, the Maryland Prince George's County Chapter of the Southern Christian Leadership Conference (SCLC) hosted a forum of black ministers and the general public. The primary objective of the forum was to discuss and brain-storm what role the black church might take in carrying out the tasks and challenges noted in the *Covenant with Black America*. The *Covenant* was a recently published book that proposed several major tasks that black people must undertake in order to move toward self-liberation.

During the forum discussions, this author presented the clergy members with a petition entitled: "No More White Gods for Black People in America." The petition requested the black clergy to stop worshipping Jesus Christ and begin worshipping only God the Creator. A copy of the petition is shown on the next page. When presenting this petition, this author stated that many of the problems experienced by young black men are due, in part, to the black clergy's leadership in the misguided worship of the white male, idol god,

Jesus Christ. This author also stated that such worship promotes a white supremacy ethos and culture that afflict black people with low self esteem, and along with other societal factors, engenders anger in many young black men who may often react with violence, delinquency, and criminal behavior.

Petition
To
Maryland Prince George's County Chapter of the Southern Christian Leadership Conference (SCLC) and
Discussion Leaders at this "Conversation about the Covenant with Black America" Thursday, May 18, 2006

No More White Gods for Black People in America

My petition to you, the members of this SCLC Discussion Board and your sponsoring organizations is that if you are serious about the contents noted in the *Covenant with Black America*, that you plan and conduct regional conferences consisting of Bible scholars, black clergy, church leaders, neighboring faith leaders, black psychologists, and sociologists who will confer and:

1. Consider and endorse the resolution (See document one) adopted in 1980 by the National Association of Black Psychologists that calls for the removal of all Caucasoid images of the Divinity from public display and from places of worship, particularly where immature black minds are likely to be exposed; and

2. Consider, endorse, and act on this author's "Appeal

to the Black Clergy" (See document two) that challenges the Black Clergy to:

a. Stop teaching the Trinitarian dogma that refers to Jesus Christ as the Son of God and the Savior of the World. This teaching is just as damaging to the psychological health of black people as the images mentioned by the black psychologists. In addition, many serious Biblical scholars have shown by detailed investigative methods that this dogma is a false faith tale that was fashioned from myths and superstitions; and

b. Begin teaching the moral and humanistic lessons that Prophet Jesus taught and emphasize that Prophet Jesus was not a Divine (a God or the Son a God), but a Jewish prophet and healer whose life story and teachings serve as good examples of how people should live and treat each other.

Enclosures

Document One: Resolution by the Association of Black Psychologists

Document Two: Appeal to the Black Clergy from Christopher Bell Jr., Ed.D.

Document One: RESOLUTION

APPROVED AT THE 1980 ANNUAL MEETING OF THE ASSOCIATION OF THE BLACK PSYCHOLOGISTS; Aug 13–16, Delaware Valley Association of Black Psychologists (Reprinted from *Chains and Images of Psychological Slavery*, ISBN 0933821-00-x), Na'im Akbar, Ph.D., New Mind Productions, .P. O Box 5185 Jersey City, NJ 07305)

WHEREAS: The portrayal of the Divine in images of Caucasian flesh constitutes an oppressive instrument destructive to the self-esteem of Black people throughout the world and is directly destructive to the psychological well-being of Black Children;

WHEREAS: The Association of Black Psychologists has condemned the negative portrayal of Blacks in media presentations in the past, we recognized the portrayal of the Divine as Caucasian as the most pervasive assertion of white supremacy. We see such grandiosity on the part of Caucasian people as destructive to themselves and damaging to people who accept white supremacy images as subliminal elements of their religious beliefs;

WHEREAS: There is a negative psychological impact when images of the Divinity and Divine figures are portrayed in Caucasian flesh with Caucasoid features, the Association of Black Psychologists considers such portrayal as being a mechanism which insidiously advocates white supremacy and by implication black inferiority;

WHEREAS: the Association of Black Psychologist, as practicing experts in human mental functioning, recognizes that the persistent exposure to such images is particularly damaging to immature Black minds;

RESOLVED: The Association of Black Psychologists recommends the removal of Caucasoid images of the Divinity from public display and from places of worship, particularly in settings where immature Black minds are likely to be exposed;

RESOLVED: That the Association of Black Psychologist provide copies of this resolution to national religious bodies, national civil rights organizations and to select religious leaders FOR THE PURPOSE OF OPENING UP AN EDUCATIONAL DIALOGUE FOR CHANGE.

Black Psychologists, National Convention, Delaware Valley Association of Black Psychologists; August 13-16, 1980, Cherry Hill Hyatt, Cherry Hill, N.J.

Document Two
Appeal to the Black Clergy
from Christopher C. Bell Jr., Ed.D.

I appeal to the Black Clergy to stop preaching and teaching black people the Trinitarian Dogma as a tenet of Faith because this dogma infers that Jesus Christ is the Son of God and is worthy to be worshipped as the Savior of the world. I make this appeal because my studies and observations for over twenty years in a variety of classroom, operational, and field teaching and learning environments have convinced me that such worship is misguided and self demeaning to black people. My studies, observations, and intuitive acumen have also convinced me that such worship promotes a white superiority syndrome (a sense of black racial inferiority), and spiritual impoverishment in many black people, and engenders an intuitive anger in many young black males. The particulars of this problem are summarized below.

a. This teaching (of the Trinitarian Dogma) is a superstitious, false-faith tale that was created and imposed beginning over 1500 years ago by the Roman emperor Constantine and his alliance of Roman Catholic Bishops. This Dogma raised Prophet Jesus to the status of an idol god the Romans named "Jesus Christ." Confessing belief in this idol god (Jesus Christ) was mandated by Roman emperors and the Catholic Church and this confession of faith was enforced by the death penalty up until the end of the middle ages.

There are many studies by Biblical scholars that detail the history of the development of the Trinitarian Dogma and the corresponding censorship, coercions, politics, torture, and deaths that the early Roman Church inflicted on those who would not "confess" belief in the teachings of the Catholic Church. Today, from an ethical perspective, the black clergy should not leave black people wallowing in ignorance about the history of this Dogma.

b. The Trinitarian Dogma portends that black men bow down and worship "Jesus Christ," who is depicted in the likeness of a white European male and white men bow down and worship their own likeness. This worship protocol is not only misguided because it promotes the worship of an idol god, "Jesus Christ," but this worship subliminally afflicts black people with a sense of low self-esteem, self-hate, anti-social attitudes, spiritual impoverishment, and a racial inferiority complex. In addition, in many young black men, this worship promotes intuitive anger and scorn toward the "whiteness worshipping" black community. Such anger and scorn are manifested as low adolescent academic achievement performance, delinquencies, drug addiction, high rates of black on black crime and mental health problems, and other behavior that may lead to incarceration.

c. Continued teaching of this Dogma subliminally promotes and nurtures a sense of superiority in pre-adolescent and adolescent white males, especially when they realize that their black counterparts are taught to believe in a "Savior" that looks like a white male. When white men are taught to believe that the savior of the world is white and sense that other people also share this belief, it is extremely difficult for them to relate to other people without a sense of superiority and the inclination to oppress and control.

d. Continued teaching of this Dogma and Creed nurtures both black and white youth about a "God" or a "Son of God" with distinctly Euro-centric physical characteristics of whiteness, beauty, thought, and holiness. Therefore this teaching will always burden black people with a sense of inferiority and uplift white people with a sense of superiority.

e. This Dogma and Creed negatively affect the psychological health of all women, including white women because it promotes the proposition that God is a white male. Not only is such a proposition unconscionable, it is inherently demeaning to the status of women in all Christian societies and gives men a godly justification to control and dominate them.

/s/ Christopher C. Bell Jr., Ed.D.

Note: Upon presentation of the petition, an

acrimonious debate ensued between the petitioner (this author) and several clergy members. The discussion leader intervened, stopped the debate, and suggested that the disputants arrange another time and place to continue their debate.

Chapter 6

The Black Clergy's response to the Petition

Introduction:

As a follow-up to the brief debate noted in the previous chapter, this author sent letters, copies of the petition, and several of the comments from the Bible scholars and black psychologists noted in Chapters 2 and 3 respectively to seven prominent black clergy members living in the Washington, DC Metropolitan Area. The letters requested these black clergy members to critique the assertions put forth in the petition and in the enclosed chapters. A copy of the letter that was sent to the clergy members is shown below.

Letter sent to Black clergy members:

Dear Reverend _____:

This letter is my request to you to review and critique the contents and conclusions noted in the attached petition, which was recently presented to clergy members who attended the Southern Christian Leadership Conference (SCLC) of Prince George's County, Maryland on May 18, 2006.

The petition is entitled "No More White Gods for Black People in White America," and requests that the SCLC take the lead to prompt the black clergy to meet regionally across the United States to discuss the necessity and means of stopping the practices of displaying images of so-called divinities and specifically to stop displaying pictures and icons of "Jesus Christ as the Son of God," and to stop the teaching of the Christian Trinitarian Dogma and Nicene Creed.

I plan to write a book on this matter and seek your input because it would be disingenuous to criticize the black clergy and not provide a forum for their counter-arguments or critique. When the book is published, you will, with your permission, be credited for your input.

If you choose to critique the petition, please limit your comments to not more than ten typewritten pages and provide your response within 45 days.

If I do not receive your reply within 45 days of sending you this letter, I will assume that you are not interested.

Sincerely,
/s/ Christopher Bell, Ed.D.
Attachments
　a/s

Response of the Black Clergy:
The letter and petition were sent by certified mail, but there was only one response from the several black clergy members, and that one response was oral. The author did not specifically obtain permission to use the

clergy member's name, but the gist of the response is summarized as follows:

Agreed that the practice of displaying pictures and icons of a white Jesus Christ as the Son of God can have and perhaps has a negative effect on black people's self-assessment and self-image and such images should be removed from churches and books and other media materials;

Noted that black churches are slowly removing such images (of white divinities), and noted that things are changing, but change takes time, especially when the images are in the stained glass windows of the church;

Asserted that when you challenge and question the origin and veracity of the Trinitarian Dogma, you are striking at the very theological foundation of the black church and this would not be helpful to black people. Black people are primarily fundamentalists. They have not heard about the Nicene Council or the Chalcedonian Council and they couldn't care less;

Asserted that from slavery to now, black people have placed their trust and faith in Jesus Christ as their God and their Lord and Savior; a Savior who is on the side of the slave and the downtrodden. Black people have historically seen themselves in the role of the oppressed and having Jesus Christ as their Lord and Savior brings them comfort. To talk against or challenge the concept of Jesus Christ as a God would not be in the best interest of black people;

Asserted that the person who makes a challenge against the Trinitarian Dogma and the Nicene Creed would be viewed as a trouble-maker or an iconoclast by the black church, and it would be more beneficial to black people if we just let sleeping dogs lie and don't stir up controversy.

The black clergy will not participate in implementing the petition.

This author's reaction to the response:

This author does not know why most of the clergy members who were contacted did not respond. However, being mindful of the vociferous argument at the SCLC forum when the petition was first presented, this author believes that the clergy members who did not respond would have sent responses that echoed the same feelings expressed in the one oral response that was received.

This author's initial reaction to the oral response was that of mixed feelings. There was a sense of buoyancy because the clergy member offered no criticism or challenge to the assertions noted in the petition. However, this author was nonplused, but not surprised when the clergy member stated words to the effect "that it would be more beneficial to black people if we let sleeping dogs lie and don't stir up controversy."

It is this author's opinion that a "let sleeping dogs lie" protocol is an unacceptable response to the petition. It is unacceptable for the following reasons:
1. The "Let sleeping dogs lie" protocol will continue to promulgate white-male worshipping folkways that endorse a "white man" to "black boy" mentality within the black community. In black people, such ethos or folkways will continue to engender feelings of low self

esteem, spiritual impoverishment, and psychological emasculation in many young black men who will intuitively resist and angrily react with violence or crime against their black communities.

2. The "Let sleeping dogs lie" action path will keep black people ignorant of themselves, ignorant of the nature of white supremacy, ignorant of the subliminal negative effects of their white-male worshipping folkways on their self esteem and spirituality, and ignorant of the history of the superstitious religious myths that direct and control their thinking. This response champions ignorance over knowledge and enlightenment and cannot in any way be beneficial to the enlightenment and psychological freedom of black people.

3. The "Let sleeping dogs lie" routine makes a statement that says: "Let's keep black people in a self-demeaning, socially subservient state of mind; let's keep them emotionally high on religion; let's keep them white-Savior-dependent and fixated on heaven and the after-life; let's keep them always feeling oppressed and downtrodden with the only relief to be found would be found in heaven. This response will ensure that black people will always cherish a loser's mentality on earth as a passport to get into heaven.

4. This author characterizes the "Let sleeping dogs lie" response not only as unacceptable from an ethical, historical, educational, and behavioral standpoint, but as a short-sighted and perhaps selfish response. This author tends to agree with Woodson (1933) who stated that those ministers who keep the people ignorant and play upon their emotion must be exiled. Woodson

noted that the people (Negroes) have never been taught what religion is, and most preachers find it easier to stimulate the superstition which develops in the unenlightened mind. Religion in such hands becomes something with which you take advantage of weak people. Why try to enlighten the people in such matters when superstition serves just as well for purposes of exploitation (p. 146).

"Children, during this summer Bible school, we'll start by introducing you to our God, Jesus Christ, your Lord and Savior."

Figure Four

Chapter 7

Where To From Here?

Introduction:

This chapter offers recommendations to black leaders and those who purport to be black leaders regarding what must be done to persuade the black clergy to stop its misguided worship protocol. This chapter is a philosophical argument for policy development that may serve as a basis for devising an action plan to convince the black clergy to stop teaching black people to worship Jesus Christ and begin teaching black people a new Christianity that espouses a *Worship only God, the source and sustainer of life* message and honors but does not worship Prophet Jesus.

The Black man's burden: a quest for psychological freedom and respected authentic manhood

There are many ways one might state the basic societal problems/challenges confronting black men in America today. Some of the possible ways of describing these challenges are: a need for full

78

employment in order to eliminate poverty; a need to raise their self esteem; a need to stop black on black crime and violence; a need to secure good education and training opportunities in order to acquire marketable skills; and a need to gain white people's respect and eliminate white racism and discrimination. These various challenges and many others, depending on the vantage point of the observer, may be used to describe the black man's major challenges. The truth of the matter is that all of these challenges have prominent places in the pantheon of challenges facing black men in America. White racism and discrimination may be two of many external societal challenges that black men encounter, but there are also serious internal (emotional, spiritual, and mental) challenges that must be addressed before external societal challenges can be solved.

This author theorizes that the black man's ultimate mental, emotional, and spiritual challenges, of which most of them may not even be aware, are to attain psychological liberation from white superiority syndrome afflictions and to establish to his own satisfaction an authentic sense of manhood.

What must black people do to address the black man's core challenges: to attain psychological liberation from white superiority syndrome afflictions and to gain an authentic sense of manhood?

As a disadvantaged people in America, black people must acquire a new sense of the world and of themselves in order to address the challenges cited above. This author suggests that these challenges must be addressed in stages.

1. The black man must ask and answer the questions: **"Who am I, and at best, who am I able to become?" Once he asks himself these questions, he must be willing to honestly plumb the depths of his own consciousness to find the answers.** Black people **must look critically at themselves** and they must be honest with what they find. Among other things, this author surmises that an honest self-inspection by black people of their social tendencies and thinking will reveal to them:

a. that they tend to cling to an abundance of negative thoughts about themselves, about their future possibilities, and about white people. **For mental therapeutic reasons, black people should attempt to discuss their negative feelings in an organized setting, either among themselves or with willing white counterparts, and attempt to shed or unburden themselves from fictitious or race-prejudice views** which they may harbor that prevent them from extending their social comfort zones toward white people or differently complexioned black people. Such discussions will allow the participants to gain a better understanding of themselves and some of the fallacies in their own thinking; an eventuality to be welcomed.

b. that they inherited (from white slave masters) a Christian belief system that gives them another white master at a higher level, a divine Jesus Christ who would be their Lord and Savior. Hopefully this revelation and black people's subsequent thoughts on this matter will prompt more questions regarding such things as "why, why not, how, who, and if" of their evaluation of their placement in their own human-valuing metrics. Such thinking will tease out answers of "who and what" black men may and can become.

2. The black man **must conquer his fear** of the white man, which means that the black man must conquer his fear of death.

3. Black clergy and secular leaders **must convene their own "Nicaea-type" councils to put an end to Constantine-certified Christianity and compose and promulgate a** *new Christianity.* *This new Christianity must espouse a "Worship only God, the source and sustainer of life" message, and honor but not worship Prophet Jesus.* Such a new version of Christianity is important to black people because it will:

a. Raise and direct their god-consciousness or sense of "the Sacred" toward those dynamisms and forces that create and sustain life and are beyond mankind's understanding. **This** *new Christianity* **would allow black people to discard all images (of persons, places and things) as representations of God and cultivate a god-consciousness wherein their "God" is too great to be comprehended and is thus beyond the conceptual grasps of the human mind;**

b. Free their minds from ancient superstitions and mythical pronouncements about virgin births, rising from the dead, bodily ascensions into heaven, walking on water, etc.;

c. End their worship of the idol Jesus Christ, but

81

openly honor Prophet Jesus as a human being and a gifted Jewish prophet, and continue teaching the morals, social ethics, and philosophy that Jesus taught;

d. Eliminate their attachment to the white-male worshipping folkways inherent in the worship of the idol Jesus Christ and thus eventually minimize and stop their subliminal, debilitating white superiority syndrome infections;

e. Eliminate the emotional and spiritual emasculation and the "boyhood" status presently imposed by Constantine-certified Christianity on many young black males as the result of the black community's white-male worshipping folkways;

f. Create or improve avenues for black men and women to learn how to become friends with less acrimony, distrust, and competition, and with more openness, and expressions of understanding.

4. The black man must meet and grapple with all of the foregoing challenges at the same time! Black people, black men in particular, must exhibit the self-discipline and self-confidence of people who are convinced that their posterity and prosperity depend on them making a change in their belief system, and in reality, such is the case.

Explaining the Black clergy's inertia:

Based on the one oral response (chapter 6) to the petition and the acrimonious exchange between the petitioner and several black clergy members during the initial presentation of the petition (chapter 5), this author's intuition and acumen presupposes that the black clergy, if left alone, would continue teaching black people to worship Jesus Christ, and would do so for the following reasons:

1. Some black clergy members may truly believe the Trinitarian Dogma and the Nicene Creed are factual accounts of what really happened in the birth, death, and after-life of Prophet Jesus. It is this author's opinion that clergy members who believe the Dogma and the Creed will never move their congregations away from a defeatist or victimized way of feeling and thinking toward a rejuvenated spirituality of yearning and questing to be self-directing, and optimistic opportunity seekers;

2. Many black clergy members may themselves be seriously afflicted with a white superiority syndrome and cannot consciously change from their white-male worshipping folkways. These black clergy members probably require their congregations to recite the Nicene Creed at Sunday worship services and will continue to do so, regardless of what they sense is true concerning the Dogma and Creed. Such clergy members become unapologetic, active propagators of the white superiority syndrome among the members of their congregations.

3. Many black clergy members may be fearful. This author suggests that their reasons for fear may fall into the following categories:

a. Many black clergy members may fear losing their prestige, income, and personal influence, and therefore will not endeavor to make a change.

b. Many black clergy members may fear reprisals from other Christians. The fear of reprisal emerges from the fact that for centuries men have killed other men because of differing religious beliefs. History provides uncontested evidence that when the majority's idea of "God's Will" is challenged the majority will strike out against the challengers. Therefore, the black clergy's fear of reprisal from other Christians is a valid concern.

Looking closer at fear:

Fear may be a valid concern, but is fear a reasonable justification for the black clergy to continue with the "Let sleeping dogs lie" worship protocol? For a partial answer to this question, this author notes the comments of Dr. Francis Welsing.

Welsing (1991) stated that an extremely high level of fear and a profound sense of vulnerability of existence can lead the human brain-computer into ineffectual patterns of circular thought. In such cases, Welsing noted, problems perceived are avoided and never solved. This is in direct contrast to effective patterns of direct linear thought that move continuously forward in straight line progress, from problem perception and depth analysis to proposed conclusive modes of problem solution. Welsing stated that circular thought means moving from problem perception, away from problem solution (down a diversionary path), and back again to problem perception. There is never consistent motion towards problem solution because to do so would challenge and alter the power dynamic of oppression.

Welsing emphasized that linear thought suggests movement from problem perception progressively toward problem solution, changing step-by-step whatever needs to be altered to achieve total problem solution, utilizing whatever means necessary to achieve this end. Black people throughout the world live under the power of the white supremacy system of total oppression and domination, implying the absence of any true power to determine ultimately what happens to their individual and collective lives. Welsing insisted that this is the major and only problem facing Blacks and all other non-white peoples throughout the world. But because this is a frightening and painful reality upon which to focus, Blacks and other non-white people, particularly in the U.S., succumb to circular thought wherein there is not only a failure to approach problem solution, but there is a stubborn refusal even to look directly at the problem (pp. 153, 154).

This author now completes the answer to the question "Is fear a reasonable justification for the black clergy to continue with the 'Let sleeping dogs lie' worship protocol," by answering "No!" Cowardliness never accomplished anything. Black men must conquer their fear, turn from their Constantine-certified Christianity, and devise a *new Christianity* that speaks to *worshipping only God, the source and sustainer of life*. If black men fail to do this, generation after generation of angry, young black men will continue their societal plight and plunge toward crime, self-abuse, low-academic achievement motivation, crime, and eventually incarceration.

A retrained, reoriented, and willing group of professionals must emerge from the ranks of those who refer to themselves as "the black clergy," and this group must assume the major role of stopping Constantine–certified Christianity and promulgating the *new Christianity*. The black clergy will not be able to do the job alone. Black secular leaders inside and outside the church must help. This reality prompts the question, "Who can help the black clergy to address the misguided worship problem?" What follows is this author's answer to this question.

Who can help the black clergy to address the misguided worship problem?

1. Can black clergy members begin to change themselves?

Yes! This author believes there are black clergy members who will agree with the arguments noted in the petition and in this book and will agree to work with others to help change the white-male worshipping folkways of black people. With this belief, this author will recommend this book to black clergy leaders and church organizations, including directors or deans of black divinity schools. Those black clergy members who are willing to make a change must gather the courage to stop their circular thinking and begin discussing the issues raised in this book. Hopefully, these discussions will be framed in terms of advantages/disadvantages of the proposed *new Christianity* versus the advantages/disadvantages of continuing the white-male worshipping folkways of Constantine-certified Christianity.

2. Can black scholars and intellectuals help the black clergy to change?

Yes! This author surveyed the writings of several notable black scholars and intellectuals to examine the solutions that they may have prescribed to enhance black self-esteem, or to move black people toward psychological liberation, or to stop the plight and societal plunge of young black men. Of the scholars and intellectuals surveyed, this author concluded that they generally:

a. Noted the need for black people to undergo or experience a cultural enlightenment or a social conversion, but none of them spoke of the specific what, when, where, or how of this cultural enlightenment or social conversion;

b. Cited poor or failing black leadership as a reason why more progress toward black psychological liberation has not been realized. However, the scholars never identified the poor or failing leadership groups and never included themselves as a part of any leadership group;

c. Did not mention, except for a very few, how the white-male worshipping folkways of Constantine-certified Christianity are self-demeaning and psychologically unhealthy to black people in general, and spiritually and emotionally emasculating to many young black men.

Nevertheless, from this survey this author sensed that there are black scholars and intellectuals whose writings suggest that they would be inclined to lend their writing skills and advocacy to help the black clergy to change from its "Let sleeping dogs lie" worship protocol, and this author will remember this book to them.

3. Can black secular community uplift organizations help the black clergy to change?

Yes! They can! However, these organizations must

understand before they become engaged in the change-making process that the black clergy must take the lead, but they (black secular organizations) must be tireless and insistent co-workers. With the idea of black secular community uplift organizations working with black clergy members, this author will recommend this book to the types of community uplift organizations shown in Appendix Four, with the hope and belief that such organizations will move forward in engaging and working with black clergy members.

4. Can black university and college students help the black clergy to change?

Yes! They can! Black male university and college students are potentially the key agents that can work with, assist, and persuade the black clergy to change its worship protocol. Black students began the lunch counter sit-ins that grew into the Civil Rights Movement. Once again, black people may have to rely on the initiative and courage of young black men to stand up and step forward. This time the standing up and stepping forward would be for the purpose of opening the closed minds of many black clergy members and thus enable these clergy members to minister to black people without holding black people hostage to fear and superstition or rendering black people vulnerable to the ravages of a white superiority syndrome.

The efforts of black university and college students should include the participation of all student organizations that are willing to work to assist the black clergy, including, ad hoc student groups, and black fraternities and sororities. With this eventually in mind, the author will ensure that student groups at historical black colleges and universities are informed of this book.

5. Can individual persons help the black clergy to change?

This is doubtful, but at a minimum, individuals should be aware of the following:

a. That the high rates of delinquencies, crime, violence, and incarceration of young black men suggest that there are factors inside the black community that obstruct or prevent the healthy personality and character development of many young black men and that this author argues that one of these factors is the misguided worship of Jesus Christ, a white male, ancient Roman idol;

b. That many black people tend to blame white racism as one of the underlying causes of the crime and violence that ravage black communities, but this author argues that often this blame falsely indicts white people and allows black people to avoid admitting their own failures. Many incarcerated young black men acquired serious anti-social personality traits and character deficiencies while maturing inside black communities where white people and white privilege have little or no direct teaching effect. This fact suggests that the black community itself is not effectively teaching (directly or subliminally) young black men what they need to know and do to avoid being incarcerated, and this author argues that one of the "harmful teachings" taking place in the black community is white male worshipping, the worshipping of Jesus Christ;

c. That many, if not most black people accept white-male worshipping as a normal way of life. Black Christians routinely perform their rituals of reciting and affirming their belief in the Nicene Creed every Sunday morning. Some black people may view this Creed as a harmless myth and others may view the Creed as a dangerous, mind-bending tenet. Nevertheless, most people remain quiet. For over a century, the silence of black people has allowed the black clergy to perpetuate this creedal ritual;

d. That one of the greatest conquering achievements of the white European male has been to use fear, intimidation, death, and propaganda to instill the image of a white male as God or as the Son of God in the minds of conquered non-white people. The imagery came with the teaching that the white male God promised a heavenly "after-life" to all who were submissive on earth to the "God-Willed" authority of the White European male and his progenies. Thus Jesus Christ, Son of God, a white, male idol was established by the Romans and later by their conquering White European progenies as a proxy or "poster personality" for over a thousand years. Thus the imagery of Jesus Christ signaled to non-white people the supremacy and godlikeness of the Western European white male.

With the above awareness, individuals will be able to understand why and how white-male worshipping, promotes the same feelings in black men as does white privilege and white racism, i.e., depression, powerlessness, low self-esteem, spiritual emasculation, racial inferiority, oppression, psychological dissonance, alienation, sullen anger, white superiority syndrome afflictions. In many young black men these feelings and afflictions tend to be psychogenic prompts for behavior that lead to recalcitrance, delinquencies, and crime.

What happens if the black clergy will not change?

If the black clergy can not be persuaded to stop its Constantine-certified Christianity and begin a *worship only God the source and sustainer of life* version of Christianity, we may expect the following:

1. Black people will continue to collectively think of themselves as members of a low caste group and inferior to white people, and unfortunately many black people will behave or act in accordance with this belief;

2. Black people will be forever burdened with a belief system that demeans them and will never allow them to free themselves from white superiority syndrome afflictions;

3. Black people will continue to think of black men as "boys" and white men as "men," and authentic black manhood will never be realized;

4. Many young black men will continue to intuitively react with anger, recalcitrance, delinquencies and criminal behavior to the disrespect, psychological emasculation, cognitive dissonance, and spiritual impoverishment subliminally imposed on them by the black community's white-male worshipping folkways, and will continue their plight and plunge toward incarceration;

5. Many black men and women will continue to experience mutual alienation in achieving trust, openness, and intimacy in their personal relationships; a situation which may, in part, be attributable to black men's subliminal jealousies about black women's emotional adorations of Jesus Christ;

6. The prospect of a "Beloved Community" of white and black people working and living together as sisters and brothers will never materialize because black people will not be able to think beyond their sense of victimization, racial inferiority, and oppression. Such a state of mind on the part of black people will not allow them the self-esteem needed to fellowship or interact as equal partners with white people, who themselves have problems of guilt and residual feelings of superiority.

7. The white supremacy philosophy of white Americans will remain strong and intact because white Americans will not have learned about or become exposed to the psychological coherence, intellectual freedom, moral prudence, and spiritual grace and harmony that would have flowed from the *new Christianity* that black people via the black clergy would have failed to initiate, and subsequently would have failed to introduce to them.

Wrap Up:
It is this author's opinion that white Americans like black Americans are in need of a spiritual rebirth and an intellectual awakening, and that the *new Christianity* recommended in this book would be a positive step in that direction. Many white clergy members will not be psychologically prepared, spiritually empowered, or socially motivated to stop the white-male worshipping protocol that has been their mythological talisman for centuries. **This means that the black clergy must bear the burden of becoming self-teachers and self-disciplinarians and commit to teaching and**

modeling the *new Christianity* to the black community and to the white clergy, who hopefully will teach the white community. Eventually most white people will embrace the *new Christianity* and America and the world will be changed for the better. The most difficult step in changing to the *new Christianity* is for black clergy and secular leaders to conquer their fear and to stop their circular thinking. The rest is easy.

You, the reader, are misled if you believe that knowledge of the truth will set you free! Knowledge of the truth merely gives you intellectual potential to act! **The attainment of psychological liberation for black people requires that they not only have knowledge of the truth, but the determination to boldly plan, and finally the moral courage to act! The psychological liberation of black people with regards to their belief system must be a self-imposed, self-administered, self-disciplined, and self deliverance process.**

Dear reader, this book has provided you and others with cogent truths regarding Constantine certified Christianity and its psychological harm to black people. Will you and the black clergy take the actions requested in this petition that would move black people toward psychological liberation? Will you help the black community to move toward a liberating *new Christianity*, or will you and the black clergy remain in place, on your knees, letting sleeping dogs lie, while trembling with fear, and the tediousness of circular thinking?

Figure Five

Epilogue

With bold clarity, this author has asserted that Jesus worship is white male worship and that such worship is deleterious, detrimental and malignant to the mental, emotional, and spiritual health of black people, especially black males. Given the high rates of recalcitrance, crime, and incarceration among many young black men, it may be said that young black men appear to be rebelling (and don't know it) against societal forces which most of us can't identify. Quite often negative societal forces are so subtly orchestrated that their existence may be unnoticed by those affected and many such forces may even be viewed as originating in their own minds. In this book, we have identified the black clergy's leadership in the worship of Jesus Christ as "white male-worshipping" that has a negative psychological effect on black people. We have argued that such worship subliminally subverts black people's functional operational thinking, diminishes their sense of self, perpetuates white superiority syndrome afflictions, and psychologically emasculates many black men.

This author has explained and petitioned the black clergy to stop leading black people in the worship of Jesus Christ and start teaching black people to worship

95

only God, the source and sustainer of life, and to honor but not worship Prophet Jesus. This author asserts that unless and until the black clergy and the black community uplift organizations act to implement his petition all other educational and social programs designed to reduce the high rates of recalcitrance, delinquencies, violence, criminal behavior, and incarcerations among young black men will be equivalent to killing barnyard crowing cocks at midnight in an attempt to hold back the sunrise.

Christopher C. Bell Jr., Ed.D.
Bell Educational Enterprises, LLC

Appendix One

Definitions of Realities (DOR):
(A discussion continuing from page 4)

Jack will do X, Y, and Z, because Jack wants to do or feels like doing X, Y, and Z. Jack will do X and Y, but not Z, because Jack wants to do or feels like doing X and Y, but not Z. But what drives Jack's wants and feelings (decision-making) about what to do? What determines how Jack thinks and feels at his decision-making time? At the conscious awareness level in non-routine matters, Jack makes decisions on how to act or behave according to how and what he feels is important (has priority), and significant (really matters) to his well-being (physical, emotional or mental). Jack also makes decisions based on his situational hazards, and his perception of the likely consequences. These personalized and situational aspects of behavioral decision-making are referred to by this author as "Definitions of Realities." **Definitions of Realities (DORs) is a construct that encapsulates the "how, what, where, why, why not, when, and ifs" that people employ to decide how to behave.** The schematic of the Black Child's Educational Environment shows a drawing of a black child with the attribute of "Definitions of Realities" which indicates that each child will react to the teaching factors in his environment based on his own unique personalized self and situational assessment. Children are not passive objects that are simply molded by the various teaching factors in their environment. As children mature, they formulate their own mental road maps of how to cope and deal with the factors in their learning environments. Children will also develop unique sets of how, what, where, why not, when, and ifs, (Definitions of Realities) (DORs) in deciding what to do or not to do. Each child's decision-making formulations (DORs) will be reflected in his attitude, personality, and behavior.

We should understand that the **black child in the schematic is faced with several teaching factors that will promote low self-esteem, cognitive dissonance, a racial inferiority complex, a sense of powerlessness, and a future outlook with diminished possibilities; however these factors do not inevitably lead that child to commit a crime or to become delinquent or violent.** On a continuing basis, each child undertakes a subconscious evaluation of his strengths and weaknesses and completes a mental mapping of the whirlwind of activities that must get his attention. The child then defines and prioritizes what he feels is important and significant in his mini-world and makes behavioral decisions accordingly. In their early teen-age years, most children begin to discern and understand their social status in the general American culture and begin acquiring a relational understanding and moral compass about what types of behavior are expected of them.

One's DORs (Definitions of realities) involve validating, analyzing, and interpreting one's experiences. DORs also involve structuring hypotheses about the self and the consequences of one's behavior. It is important to understand that Definitions of Realities (DORs) are decision making tools that encompass an individual's self-image, feelings, past experiences, visionary impulsions, repertoire of adaptive skills, internal motivational intensity, moral outlook, beliefs, and the situational environment.

Upon entering kindergarten, all children's Definitions of Realities have already been provided a frame of reference via the DORs of their parents. Black parents, as do all parents, provide their children with their best possible parental raw materials from which to build pleasant, happy, and visionary DORs. In this regard, black parents' tasks differ from white parents' tasks in intensity and focus, because black parents recognize that their children's learning environment is often hostile and White parents do not have the same concerns regarding their children's learning environment.

For further elaboration on DORs, the author refers the reader to Bell's (1986) unpublished thesis cited below.

Citation: ED 266234: <u>Explaining the Progressively Decreasing Scores on Comprehensive Tests of Basic Skills (CTBS) of the School Children of the District of Columbia Public Schools as They Progress from</u>

<u>Elementary School into High School;</u> <u>(1986),</u> (Bell, Christopher, Jr.). This unpublished thesis may be obtained from the Education Resources Information Center (ERIC).

Appendix Two

Understanding the White Superiority Syndrome
(A discussion continuing from page 5)

In his book, *The Belief Factor and the White Superiority Syndrome,* Bell (2000) described the White Superiority Syndrome (WSS) as the internalized belief that white people as a group are inherently, genetically, and esoterically better human beings than black people. Bell noted that this syndrome develops subliminally in both white people and black people, especially if they have internalized a white-male, god consciousness. People who have acquired this syndrome are characterized by a way of thinking that supports the notion that whites should control and direct, and blacks and others should follow. People with this syndrome also believe whites should set the standards, mores, and values for all things that are dear and important to the culture. They believe further that persons with physical features approximating white norms (light skin, straight hair, narrow nose, etc.) are to be valued higher than those who are farther removed from those physical white norms. Bell noted that a white person does not have to show hate toward black people as an indicator of having acquired a White Superiority Syndrome. If a white person thinks or feels that he is better than black people by virtue of his white skin, that white person has acquired the White Superiority Syndrome (p. 29).

Bell stated that White Superiority Syndrome afflictions are characterized by the following thinking patterns:

Thinking patterns of black people who are afflicted with a White Superiority Syndrome.

1. God gave the world to the white man to rule.
2. Hatred and fear of white people.
3. Profound jealousy of white people.
4. General dislike of dark-skin black people, including themselves, if they have dark skin.
5. Inhibition or avoidance toward competing with white people in academic challenges and intellectual pursuits.
6. Believing that lighter skin and straight hair are the ideal.
7. Thinking that brains and intelligence come mostly with whiter skin.
8. Thinking: If you're white, you're all right; if you're brown, stick around; but if you're black, stay back!
9. Self-talking: I hope Jesus doesn't penalize me because I'm black.
10. Self-talking: There's God, but he must not like black people too much.
11. Thinking: Yeah, I'm a nigger and everybody knows that a nigger ain't nothing.
12. Reasoning: God is white, because Jesus is White. This means whites are closer to God than blacks.

13. Self-talk: I can't do it; the white man won't let me!
14. Feelings: I hate white people. They're evil.
15. Self-talk: There's no need to try. I'm Black!
16. Self-talk: I'm lighter than she is and that means I am better.
17. Self-talk: I ain't nothing but a nigger, let's face it.
18. "So you're studying, eh. You trying to be white?"
19. This child (new born baby) is dark. He stayed in the oven (womb) too long.
20. Why try? The white man is going to end up being boss.
21. When I think about God, I can close my eyes and see Jesus.
22. The white man's ice is colder than the colored man's ice.
23. Never trust a Nigger!
24. Let's dress her like an angel; let her wear the blond wig.
25. The white Barbie doll is prettier than the brown Barbie doll.

<u>Thinking patterns of white people who are afflicted with a White Superiority Syndrome</u>
1. Negroes ought to be shipped back to Africa.
2. All that blacks want to do is to get on welfare.
3. We whites are better looking and more intelligent than black people.
4. We whites should be in charge; don't forget it.
5. Why waste money on black education. Nothing's going to make them improve.
6. We whites should have priority. We deserve it!
7. Blacks are habitual trouble makers; it's part of their

make up.

8. I'll help them. These black people are so like children.

9. I don't like them and don't want to be around them because they don't look clean.

10. Everybody knows that niggers ain't nothing, and they know it too.

11. An educated nigger is still a nigger.

12. When I think about God, I can close my eyes and see a Jesus, who looks a lot like me.

13. I have no problems with Negroes and I get along fine with them as long as they know their place.

14. The white Barbie doll is prettier than the brown Barbie doll (pp. 29, 30).

Appendix Three

Concerning Black Male Authentic Manhood
(A discussion continued from page 11)

As used in this book, *authentic manhood* refers to black males' healthy, ego-enhancing, self-esteem as demonstrated by their age-appropriate, responsible behavior, and their questing to be the best of what they earnestly wish themselves to be or become.

It is an historical fact, that during slavery, Negro male slaves could not exert their manhood because they would have been judged as "bad niggers" and slaughtered by their white slave masters. Slavery's harsh treatment and torture were physical deterrents that prevented Negro male slaves from exhibiting authentic manhood, except among themselves via physical feats or extra-ordinary labor.

The white slave master gave the ancient Roman, Constantine-certified, version of Christianity to the Negro slave. This version of Christianity presented the Negro slave with an additional and higher level of white male dominance: that of a white male, son of God, Jesus Christ, who was the Lord and Savior of the world. Coupled with the harshness and inhumane culture of the Institution of Chattel Negro Slavery, this version of Christianity became a formidable psychological and spiritual deterrent to the Negro male slave's impulse to exhibit authentic manhood. This version of Christianity set the precedence and psychological stage for the mature Negro male to be thought of by both white and black people as a "boy" when comparing him to mature white men.

It is easy to understand that the Negro male slave's adoption of and adaptation to the slave master's Christianity was a necessary and smart thing to do in order to survive and gain the slave master's trust. Thus, in spite of the self-demeaning and servile requirements, the negro male slave adopted and used the Constantine-certified version of Christianity to search for and find solace, and to gather hope for a better life with Jesus Christ, a heavenly, white, humane master.

However, a century and a half after the end of slavery, black men in America continue to accept and embrace the slave master's Constantine-certified version of Christianity via the black clergy's worship leadership. It is this author's opinion that the Constantine-certified version of Christianity is in essence "white-male worshipping," and that white-male worshipping folkways negatively affects black male authentic manhood as follows:

1. **White-male worshipping folkways subliminally diminished the urge in many older black men to exhibit authentic manhood traits** as compared to similarly aged white men. Over their lifetime, older

black men have been indoctrinated with a white superiority syndrome and have adopted a "leave it alone" or "what's the use in trying" frame of mind when confronted with white racism. These older black men have stopped thinking about saving themselves and others from the servility and belittlements required of them by the Constantine-certified version of Christianity. The saving grace for most of these older black men is that they are not aware of the villainous role that their belief system has played in their lack of authentic manhood and in their acquiescence, nervousness, and meekness when they come face to face with white men.

2. White-male worshipping folkways emotionally emasculate and promote anger and disdain in many young black men. In many young black men, the white-male worshipping folkways of their black communities promote low self-esteem, and feelings of being disrespected, effeminized, and devalued. Upon becoming consciously aware of the fact that a white male is presented to them as their Lord and Savior, many young black men just stay away from church in order to avoid the self-demeaning and servility of white-male worshipping. Other young black men will not just stay away from church but will act out their subliminal, sullen anger and sense of emasculation with recalcitrance, delinquencies, violence, self-abuse, and criminal behavior.

The social and economic structures in America today still present a view of black males as *boys* and white males as *men*. These structures are promoted and underwritten by Constantine-certified Christianity. As

107

we have noted earlier, being unable to realize their authentic manhood in comparison to white men, many young black men tend to seek their manhood by abusing their spouses, oppressing black women by force or rule setting, fathering children out of wedlock, and engaging in bizarre activities that bring them notoriety.

3. White male worshipping folkways promote alienation between black men and women. During weekly Sunday church services, many black women emotionally shout praises and adorations for Jesus Christ as if Jesus Christ were their physical lover. Their adorations and joyous shouts entreat Jesus Christ to come to them and take them into the safety of his arms and delivery them from their earthly woes (and away from the weak black "boys" surrounding them). When black women shout worshipful expressions of love and adoration toward a white male image (Jesus Christ), real or imagined, the two-some relationship that might exist between a black woman and a black man mutates into a troublesome three-some relationship that now includes Jesus Christ, the black woman's god and simulated lover. It is this author's opinion that the black woman's enthusiasm in loving and praising Jesus Christ mediates downward the chances of the healthy development of mutual respectfulness, honesty, openness, intimacy, and equanimity between black women and black men.

To emphasize this point, this author again asks, **"If people all over the world worshipped a white, blond, female as 'Our Lady and Savior of the World,' what would be the nature of the worshipful** adorations offered during Sunday morning worship services, by whom, and how would such 'white-female worshipping' affect the relationships between black men and women?"

Appendix Four

Concerning Black Secular Community Uplift Organizations
(A discussion continued from page 88)

At a minimum, this author will contact major black clergy and church organizations, black university and college Schools of Divinities, and black secular community up-lift organizations of the types listed below and make them aware of the contents of this book. The author will also make them aware of the need for them to assist the black clergy to stop the misguided worship of Jesus Christ, and begin teaching black people a *new Christianity, such* as we have discussed in this book.

Typical secular uplift organizations to be contacted:

- Greek and Professional Black Fraternities
- Greek and Professional Black Sororities
- Greek fraternities at Black Historical Universities
- Greek sororities at Black Historical Universities
- Children's Defense Fund

- National Urban League
- National Association for the Advancement of Colored People
- National Association of African American Studies
- Blacks in Government
- National Forum for Black Public Administration
- Congress of Racial Equality
- Rainbow Push Coalition
- On Wheels Inc
- American Council of Education
- Conference of Minority Public Administrator
- National Minority Business Council
- Smithsonian Institution
- National Association of Minority Media Executives
- Linkage, Inc
- National Council of Negro Women, Inc
- Black Enterprise Magazine
- 100 Black Men of America, Inc
- National Conference of Black Mayors
- National Association of Black Owned Broadcasters
- National Newspaper Publisher Association
- Southwest Center for Human Relations
- National Council of Negro Women
- National Black Law Student Association
- Congressional Black Caucus Foundation
- Progressive National Baptist Convention, Inc

Christopher C. Bell Jr., Ed.D.

- Association for the Study of African American Life and History
- National Black Child Development Institute
- National Alliance of Black School Educators
- National Black Caucus of State Legislators

References

Akbar, Na'im. <u>Chains and Images of Psychological Slavery</u>. Jersey City, NJ. New Mind Productions, 1991

Baigent, Michael. <u>The Jesus Papers.</u> New York, New York, HarperCollins Publishers, 2006

Bell, Christopher. <u>The Belief Factor and the White Superiority Syndrome.</u> Bloomington, IN: 1St Books Library, 2001

Clark, Kenneth. <u>Dark Ghetto</u>. New York, New York, Harper and Row, 1967

Ehrman, Bart.D. <u>Lost Christianities.</u> Oxford, New York, Oxford University Press, 2005

Fishbein, Martin & Icek, Ajzen. <u>Belief, Attitude, Intention and Behavior.</u> Reading, MA: Addison-Wesley Publishing Co., 1975

Funk, Robert W. <u>Honest to Jesus: Jesus for a New Millennium.</u> New York, New York, Polebridge Press, 1996

Grier, William & Cobb, Price. <u>Black Rage</u>. New York, New York, Basic Books, 1992

Jones, James A. "Politics of Personality: Being Black in America," in <u>Black Psychology.</u> (Edited by Reginal L. Jones), Berkeley CA, Cobb and Henry Publishers, 1991

Kunjfu, Jawanza. <u>Adam! Where Are you?</u> Chicago, Ill, African American Images, 1994

Ludemann, Gerd. <u>The Resurrection of Christ: An Historical Inquiry</u>, Amherst, New York, Prometheus Press, 2004

Sergiovanni, Thomas & Starratt, Robert. <u>Emerging Patterns of Supervision: Human Perspectives,</u> New York, NY: McGraw Hill Book Company, 1971

Spong, John Shelby. <u>A New Christianity for a New World</u>, New York, HarpersCollins Publishers, 2002

The Smiley Group, Inc. <u>Covenant with Black America,</u> Chicago, Ill: The Third World Press, 2006

The Jesus Seminar. <u>The Five Gospels</u>, New York, New York, A Polebridge Press Book, 1993

Turner, Rodgers D. "Moving Toward Realistic Explanations and Solutions," in <u>Black on Black Crime.</u> (Edited by P. Ray Kedia), Bristol, IN, Wyndhamn Hall Press, 1994

Welsing, Francis. The Isis Paper; Keys to the Colors. Chicago, Ill: The Third World Press, 1991

Wilson, Amos. Black on Black Violence. New York, New York, African World Infosystems, 1990

Woodson, Carter G. The Mis-education of the Negro. Washington, DC: The Associate Publishers Inc., 1933

ABOUT THE AUTHOR

Christopher C. Bell Jr., Ed.D., Major, U.S. Army Retired, is a seasoned educationist and veteran observer and analyst of the motivational and behavioral effects of religious educational programs on black people. Dr. Bell has developed, managed, monitored, and evaluated educational and motivational training programs in the U.S. Army, the U.S. Department of Labor, the District of Columbia Public School System, and the U.S. Department of Education. Dr. Bell is a graduate of Virginia State University (B.S.) and Fitchburg State University (M.Ed.). He earned a Certificate of Advance Studies (C.A.S.) from Harvard University Graduate School of Education and a Doctor of Education (Ed.D.) degree from Boston University Graduate School of Education.